A Season of
SINGLENESS

Ray E. Larson

Gospel Publishing House/Springfield, Mo. 65802

02-0584

Unless otherwise noted, all Scripture quotations in this book are from *The Holy Bible: New International Version,* © 1978 by the New York International Bible Society. Used by permission of Zondervan Bible Publishers.

© 1984 by the Gospel Publishing House, Springfield, Missouri 65802. All rights reserved. No part of this book may be reproduced, stored in a retrieval system, or transmitted in any form or by any means—electronic, mechanical, photocopy, recording, or otherwise—without prior written permission of the copyright owner, except brief quotations used in connection with reviews in magazines or newspapers.

Library of Congress Catalog Card Number 83-81762
International Standard Book Number 0-88243-584-1
Printed in the United States of America

To those whom God has allowed me the privilege of pastoring, whose lives have shaped the message of this book.

To my wife Rebecca, whose life is on every page.

Acknowledgments

I would like to express my thanks to Laurie Warner who assisted in the completion of this book. A special thanks to Bobbie Reed, who read, reread, and edited the manuscript.

I appreciate those who have been a part of the Christian Singleness and Relationship seminars, which is the foundation of this book.

Most of all, I must acknowledge the believers of Praise Celebration and His Place Christian Fellowship whose lives have shaped this book.

Foreword

Ray Larson has helped hundreds of single people to adapt to their status in life. His insights into the particular needs of singles give him credibility.

As a member of the staff of Capital Christian Center in Sacramento, California, Pastor Larson is ministering on a weekly basis, along with his wife, Becky, to at least one-third of the congregation. His Monday night "celebration" for singles has become a lifeline for hundreds.

As you read *A Season of Singleness* you will detect the sincerity and compassion of Ray Larson. Those traits that were so evident in our Lord Jesus are transmitted through yielded vessels on earth. Ray Larson is such a vessel. May you be blessed and helped as you share his insights in the pages to follow.

GLEN D. COLE
SENIOR PASTOR
CAPITAL CHRISTIAN CENTER

Contents

Introduction 9
1. Single! 11
2. Singlephobia and "The Weirdness" 15
3. Learning To Be a Satisfied Single Man 25
4. Becoming a Contented Single Woman 31
5. A Season of Singleness 39
6. Fulfilled in Him 46
7. Are You Ready for Company? 53
8. Mending Relationships 62
9. Caring and Sharing 70
10. Successful Dating 81
11. Finding *the* One 101
12. Living Abundantly 107

Introduction

So you're single. The success of the single life-style, whether short or long, depends largely on one's attitude about it.

The struggle to be satisfied in singleness is often complicated by the church's attitude toward the single adult. In the past, church leaders and members have made the mistake of rejecting singleness as an adequate life-style. Many individuals have launched personal crusades to stamp out the problem in their local church by either publicly demeaning singleness or having matchmaking activities for the unmarried.

Times are changing. One writer tells us that 42 percent of the adult population is single. The church has begun to accept singleness as normal and is beginning to implement ways to meet the growing needs of the single person.

As a single person, you must come to grips with your attitudes about your present circumstances. God intends for your life to be rich and complete, full of meaningful experiences—both as a single person and in your relationships. Your ability to know all God has in store for your life *right now* depends on how you respond to your own situation.

A Season of Singleness provides guidelines for the unmarried person to experience an exciting life in God.

It helps make today all that God intends it to be for singles. This book will consider practical steps for both living your individual life and relating to the opposite sex.

As a pastor, I have watched singles put the principles of *A Season of Singleness* into practice. Hundreds of singles are sharing life together and, with the help of the church, lessening the game playing and fleeing from singleness. These singles are letting God control their lives, living for today—confident God will guide their tomorrows. They share *agape* love with the opposite sex in a life-changing way without being involved in a shallow relationship.

No matter how long you're in it, your season of singleness can be God's tool to give you His completeness.

1
Single!

Several hands went up in the group as the speaker asked people to share how they felt about being single. "I want to get married," one man stated simply. "Out-of-place. It's a couple's world," a woman shared. "Most of the time it's okay, but sometimes very lonely," another young man confessed. "Scarey," someone called out, and several heads nodded in agreement.

The Myths

The way you feel about being single, or single again, will depend on what you believe about singleness. And because there are several popular myths about singleness, many people do not accept it in their lives. Let's examine the myths.

Everyone should get married

If everyone should get married, then being single becomes the waiting room for marriage. Therefore, the objective is to be single for as short a time as possible, and spouse hunting becomes one's main interest. People who accept this myth begin to develop a sense of desperation if they don't find a suitable mate within a certain period of time. The longer they are single the more focused their attention becomes on getting married.

Because they believe that everyone should get married, some people never learn to be self-reliant. So, as singles, they are usually dependent on other people for some things, and frequently frustrated by their own inabilities. "If I only had a husband," one woman explained angrily as she kicked the flat tire on her car in the parking lot, "I wouldn't have to worry about these things!"

There's something wrong with you if you're not married

This second myth stems from the first and is perpetuated by the familiar query, "So, how come a nice guy/gal like you isn't married?" Finally, we begin to wonder ourselves. If no one loves us, then we must be unlovable. And when we feel unlovable, we cannot develop a positive self-image, or risk reaching out to others. The result is either withdrawal and depression, or an attempt at an image of lovableness, hoping someone will be fooled. Usually no one is.

Being single is the worst possible alternative

People who accept this third myth will grasp at any relationship available, and marry as soon as possible. Even a bad relationship is perceived as better than no relationship at all. Marriage is expected to be an instant and permanent cure for loneliness, immaturity, and unhappiness. It isn't of course.

Being single is a guarantee of not being hurt again

Some people who have lost a spouse through death or divorce decide to remain single for the rest of their lives so they won't be hurt again. While they may appear to have accepted singleness, they are actually hiding out in fear. They will not let people get too close and consequently they are truly lonely.

Only a spouse can meet my needs

Those who think that only a mate can meet their needs for affirmation, love, attention, and fellowship do not develop strong social networks. They have few friendships, most fairly casual. Assuming no responsibility for taking care of their own emotional needs, these people are always waiting for someone to come along and make them happy.

The Problem With Myths

The problem with accepting myths such as these is that you are prevented from accepting a healthy concept of being single. These myths cause people to have poor self-images and to sacrifice the present for an *imaginary future.*

The Bible tells us that we are not to live for tomorrow because we have no guarantee about the events of tomorrow (James 4:14,15). Today is all we can count on. And we are accountable for how we spend the "today" we do have.

Take a few minutes to consider your own beliefs about being single by completing the following sentences. Quickly write several endings for each sentence without giving them much thought.

1. Because I'm single, I feel . . .
2. Singleness is . . .
3. I hate being single when . . .
4. One good thing about being single is . . .
5. Because I'm single, I can't . . .
6. People think that singles are . . .

7. I'd be okay with my singleness if . . .

8. Most people should get married by the time they are . . .

9. Being single at my age was/was not what I expected it to be because . . .

10. I'm uncomfortable being single when . . .

When you have finished, review what you've written and see if you can pick out some beliefs you have about being single at this time in your life. Are your beliefs mainly positive or negative? Can you think of any examples of how your thoughts about being single have influenced your actions or attitudes? You probably can.

It's Okay To Be Single!

Every person is single for some portion of his life. For some it is only a short time, the first 17 to 21 years; for others it is most of their lives. But we all have a season of singleness. It is good. It is useful. There is a purpose for being single.

If we can accept this purpose, then we can accept our singleness and be comfortable with not being married. We can find new ways to live a committed life, and experience a new level of joyous Christian fellowship. Being single can become an adventure of exploration of God's will for our lives. Letting go of the myths may not be easy, but it is essential if we are to live an abundant life.

So, don't be like some people who insist on clinging to the myths, and consequently develop an irrational fear of being single for any length of time.

2
Singlephobia and "The Weirdness"

George and Mary met at a singles group one night and were married four weeks later.

Karen became deeply depressed when a casual relationship broke up.

Carl begs God every morning to bring a mate into his life.

So many single adults seem to suffer from *singlephobia*: an irrational, excessive fear of being single. To understand this fear, think of other phobias people may have: claustrophobia, fear of being in a confined, close space; or acrophobia, fear of high places. A person with claustrophobia may do anything to avoid being confined, such as walking up 31 flights of stairs rather than riding in a small elevator. The person with acrophobia may do neither, because any meeting held 31 floors off the ground is obviously not worth attending!

However, should a phobic person be unexpectedly caught in the circumstance he fears, his one thought is to escape. He becomes increasingly panicked and irrational until he is out of the situation. Thus a person with singlephobia may go to great lengths to escape being single.

This strange emotional disorder begins to take over the affected person's thinking. He becomes obsessed with getting married, and begins a frantic search for a close relationship that might lead to marriage. In fact, any member of the opposite sex is approached as a prospective life partner. The hunt is on. Tallyho!

Soon, not only are his relationships affected but so is every aspect of his life. Escaping singleness is all he talks about. A singlephobic eats, drinks, sleeps (dreams), lives, and prays *marriage.*

God's Sovereignty

The problem with becoming singlephobic lies in the fact that an irrational, excessive fear of being single displaces one's trust in the sovereignty of God. Jesus told us not to worry, saying rather to "seek first his kingdom and his righteousness" (Matthew 6:33). He was thinking about our being preoccupied with *daily needs,* the *essentials* of life. So how much more we ought to heed His admonition when we become obsessed with a secondary need in life.

Besides, our Heavenly Father knows our needs and He performs well in meeting them. He can perform equally well as a matchmaker. After all, God has had a lot of experience selecting mates. Remember Adam and Eve—Isaac and Rebekah—Boaz and Ruth?

Most of us have a deep desire to love and be loved by a person of the opposite sex. Desiring marriage is not wrong in itself. The desire becomes wrong when it becomes an obsession, causing us to doubt the Lord's timing, and to take matters into our own hands. Our thoughts become focused on the matrimonial objective, and consequently are not centered on the Lord Jesus Christ. Yet Paul tells us "If then you were raised with Christ, seek those things which are above. . . . Set your mind on things above, not on things on the earth" (Colossians 3:1,2, NKJV). So persons who are experiencing singlephobia need to regain control of their thought lives, and seek opportunities to serve Jesus.

Ironically, when people are terrified of being single and are always looking for permanent relationships, the relationships they do have tend to suffer. Friendships that are not perceived as potential dating relationships are discarded. And the expectations in any dating relationships are so unrealistic that they often do not survive either. The joy is gone from the interactions in relationships because of the pressure to find a mate.

The tragedy is that so many singlephobics inhabit our world that they frequently find each other and get married quickly, often to their eventual sorrow. But when we remember that our God is sovereign, and omniscient, we can trust in His timing and His guidance of our lives. God knows when—or if—we truly need a marriage relationship. Allowing God to bring the right persons into our lives at the right time and committing the development of loving relationships to His divine plan are guarantees of a successful life.

And yet, some people become impatient with God's plan and timing. Out of their singlephobia emerges a strange set of symptoms I call the "weirdness."

Two Types of the Weirdness

The weirdness can take two forms: total weirdness and specific weirdness.

Total weirdness is a preoccupation with immediate marriage, to someone—anyone! Specific weirdness is a preoccupation with immediate marriage to a specific person—whether or not that person wants to.

While I was attending Bible college I saw several future preachers (including me) suffering from total weirdness. Believing that we had to be married before entering full-time ministry, we walked around campus, our eyes wide open, searching for that perfect potential preacher's wife. The closer we came to graduation, the more frantic the search.

As a senior, I became so afraid of graduating wifeless that I threw myself headlong into an extensive search for a mate. My fear of being single showed. I was desperate. Dating became uncomfortable. My search was unsuccessful because my total weirdness scared people away.

Of course, you don't have to be a pastor-in-training to have the total weirdness. Anyone can exhibit the symptoms. It is especially obvious in singles who get involved with a different person every week, endlessly striving to find someone who fits the qualifications on their shopping lists.

When a potential mate is spotted, the total weirdness can change into specific weirdness as one's fantasies are immediately rewritten to embrace that person as a loving partner. Sometimes this occurs without even an introduction to one another; you know, love at first *sight*.

Usually when we have specific weirdness we want to validate our plans, so we say, "Aha! We enjoy being together. We meet each other's requirements in a mate. Obviously, then, this person is God's will for me!" And so we proceed to develop the relationship as though God had ordered us to start making marriage plans (the sooner, the better).

During Bible college, Eric had a critical case of specific weirdness. He met a girl who was exactly what he thought he desired. He knew right away that he wanted to marry her. So, when they started dating, he told his friends that she was going to be his wife. He took her home to meet his family, and started to make marriage plans. A few months later D day arrived, and she ended their relationship. Eric was embarrassed, and shocked by her spiritual insensitivity and inability to hear God's voice as he did. He was shattered for weeks.

Obviously, Eric hadn't heard God's voice at all, but only the siren call of the specific weirdness. It is amazing how often we interpret our own feelings as being the voice of the Lord. The beautiful thing about God's will is that when we commit our lives to Him, He can be trusted to work out all the details. We don't have to force someone to love or marry us!

If God cares enough about us to provide for our physical needs, as we have already noted, will He not also provide for our emotional needs? And God knows exactly how those needs can best be met. For some people a relationship with a spouse can fulfill those needs. For others, their greatest fulfillment may lie in singleness.

Have You Got the Weirdness?

Take a few minutes and check yourself for symptoms of the weirdness.

Is communicating with the opposite sex difficult?

When a relationship is centered in Christ, and our emotions are in submission to the Holy Spirit, we are at ease around members of the opposite sex. We can share our feelings, our ideas, our lives, and talk about the purpose of that relationship. However, when our emotions are influenced by the weirdness, we become manipulative and superficial, even dishonest, in our sharing, because we are afraid of being rejected.

In my own experience with the specific weirdness I was dismayed at my hesitancy to be open. The purpose of our relationship became uncertain and confusing to the girl I was dating. And, as with all relationships in which a communication breakdown is not mended, the end was inevitable.

Do I spend an inordinate amount of time daydreaming about marriage?

Planning for marriage is an appropriate activity for engaged couples. But spending long hours fantasizing about marriage before you have even a serious dating relationship is a pretty strong indication that you have the weirdness!

Charles was attracted to a visitor in the singles Sunday school class one morning. However, being shy, he left without getting acquainted. That afternoon he started daydreaming about meeting her, falling in love instantly, and getting married. He drove to the shopping mall, and walked by jewelry stores, mentally selecting the wedding rings they might buy. Later he drove through a nice section of the city where he had always wanted to live when he got married. Charles even wrote down the telephone number of the real estate agent for a couple of the houses which were for rent in that area. Charles was suffering an acute case of the weirdness!

"I remember when I was having problems with the weirdness," said Mark. "I would sometimes meet a girl and drift off into daydreams of walking down the aisle together, owning a house, making it especially our own, having a family and sharing in the ministry together. I was terribly embarrassed one day when a girl asked me, 'Why are you staring at me?'

"What was I supposed to say, 'Oh, I was just thinking of our wedding day!'? She would have dropped me right then! I had no right to start thinking about marriage when we had just met. I was trying to force the relationship."

Do I avoid the person I daydream about?

If you have the weirdness for someone, you often don't know how to deal with the problem. Consequently, you may start to avoid meeting or being with that person. Teenagers walk down the hallway toward one another, suddenly spot each other, then turn around and go the opposite direction. What they really want more than anything else is to be together. Adults may do the same, spending time actually avoiding the person they want to be with.

Am I anxious or nervous?

Frequently the weirdness is accompanied by nervousness. Sweaty palms are one sign of nervousness, especially in zero degree weather. Another is a loss of appetite. You go out to dinner on a date, order a big meal, then sit there unable to eat it because of the butterflies in your stomach. You become tense and anxious about saying and doing the right things. Insomnia can be another sign of nervousness if you lie awake at night pondering the next conversations and painting mental pictures of future good times together.

Have priorities changed?

The most dangerous symptom of the weirdness is allowing your priorities to shift so that marriage, or that special someone, becomes the priority of your life. Jesus Christ is to have that preeminence (Colossians 1:18). We are told "Love the Lord your God with all your heart and with all your soul and with all your mind" (Matthew

22:37). Of course, Satan delights in distracting your mind from God, the Word, prayer, and ministry in order to lessen your effectiveness for the Kingdom.

Am I clinging to an unhealthy relationship?

Often people with the total weirdness will reason that any relationship is better than no relationship. So they cling to any relationship they have—even unhealthy ones—just so they won't be alone. What they don't realize is that as long as they are in an unhealthy relationship, they are *unavailable* for a healthy relationship! Also, they are using people for selfish purposes.

How To Cure the Weirdness

The weirdness is a result of selfishness. Like spoiled children begging for candy, we want to have a relationship, and we want to have it *now!* Such an obsession is not only unbiblical; it is emotionally unhealthy. We may *think* we are loving someone by wanting to marry him or her, but for the Christian outside of God's will such impulses are likely more selfish than loving. That person becomes little more than an object of love; someone with whom to be married. We are in love with love, or marriage, not that person.

Marriage was never meant to be an end in itself. It is an avenue of expressing love. Marriage should be a demonstration of the ultimate love. Instead, the National Center for Health Statistics indicates that for every two couples getting married today there is another couple getting a divorce. And that disheartening statistic includes Christians—even ministers. The divorce rate for this latter group, according to one source, "has at least quadrupled since 1960."[1] What is wrong?

For one thing we are bombarded with false impressions about marriage from the media, especially television. We see glamour-girl wives in silk nightgowns and virile, bare-chested husbands. The handsome couple awakens from a night's sleep with every hair in place. Except for the sake of humor, we rarely see the wife with curlers in her hair and cold cream on her face, the husband with his hair on end and his paunch out of place! That is closer to the norm. We are promised a perfect relationship if we use the right shampoo, mouthwash, or soap. All of the media's false impressions help create an environment congenial to the propagation of the weirdness virus.

And yet marriage is not the fantasy perpetuated by the media. It is a real relationship that takes work to develop. It is giving, not just receiving. And the giving must be 100 percent, expecting nothing in return. If we honestly understood and accepted the Biblical concept of true servanthood in marriage many of us would not fantasize so much about marriage.

To be cured of the weirdness, you must be very honest with yourself. First, recognize the problems, and admit that you are in love with the idea of marriage. Then, be willing to confess that attitude to the Lord, and repent. Surrender to Him your desire to be married. Ask God to help you learn to be content as a single adult.

Paul challenges us to be followers of his example, saying, "I have learned to be content in whatever circumstances I am" (Philippians 4:11, NASB). And he encourages us in 1 Timothy 6:6 by pointing out that "godliness with contentment is great gain" (KJV).

We must come to the place where we are no longer singlephobic. As long as we are afraid of being single, we are susceptible to the weirdness! Eileen remembers thinking that singleness was a terrible curse, but now, in retrospect, she praises God for those years and the many special opportunities God gave her because she was single.

If you are struggling with singlephobia, cry out to God, "for he will deliver the needy who cry out" (Psalm 72:12). And most of all, rather than pursuing marriage, pursue pure love. Peter says, "Now that you have purified yourselves by obeying the truth so that you have sincere love for your brothers, love one another deeply, from the heart" (1 Peter 1:22).

Truly loving one another means desiring the other's highest good, not our own. No emotional game playing. It means serving, not demanding. It means helping one another seek God's will. Pure love for our brothers and sisters in Christ is the cure for the weirdness.

Finally, become content in your relationship with the Lord. Learn to trust him in all areas of your life. With His help regain control over your thought life; ". . . take captive every thought to make it obedient to Christ" (2 Corinthians 10:5). Eliminating the weirdness from our lives opens the door for great relationships as single Christians. No longer is everyone we meet a prospective partner, but a new brother or sister in the Lord.

---

[1]*Christianity Today,* February 5, 1982, Vol. 26, no. 3, p. 20.

3
Learning To Be a Satisfied Single Man

I've always been a romantic at heart. Watching screen romances, I would identify readily with the leading man as he attempted to win the heart and hand of the leading lady. Little wonder that relationships with girls were very important to me during my junior and senior high school years. Going steady guaranteed me dates on the weekends, and between girl friends I made every attempt to book dates with several girls.

A Friday or Saturday night without a date meant that I was a failure. And I hated that feeling! So, I worked hard at keeping a steady girl friend. Copying my heroes, I'd take my dates out to dinner and gaze soulfully into their eyes. I sent romantic cards, and brought flowers.

I kept trying to find the one special relationship which would be "happily ever after."

During my sophomore year of high school, I became a Christian, and not long after that I felt God's call into the ministry. So after graduation I entered Southern California College as a student of pastoral studies. It was during college that I became even more acutely aware that I was *single*!

No Singleness Allowed!

Singles are often considered to be in a state of limbo,

anxiously awaiting marriage as a panacea for spiritual ineffectiveness. Married Christians tend to think that something must be wrong in the spiritual lives of their single friends. Surely, they cannot possibly be in the center of God's will.

Marriage is viewed, and thus unwittingly taught, as the ultimate life-style. If marriage is the only reasonable life-style in the church, what happens to the many single believers who are trying to serve the kingdom of God? Marriage certainly is in God's plan for man, but thankfully, the church is awakening to see that singleness has a significant role as well.

While single myself, I felt as though I were wandering in the wilderness, waiting to enter the Promised Land of marriage. The pressures placed on me to find a mate became most intense during college. While I was visiting home one weekend, a sweet, elderly lady in the church spoke sincerely to me. "You will be in the ministry soon. Why don't you have a wife yet? I would not want you to enter the ministry and be ineffective. I am going to intercede for you in prayer."

Wow! There I was, excitedly preparing for pastoral ministry, and a godly prayer warrior tells me I would be ineffective without a wife.

The search was on! I became paranoid, a nervous hunter on safari for a wife! I developed the disease, *singlephobia*. Eligible young women, however, could sense my anxiety about finding a wife and subsequently avoided me as they would a leper. My search was self-defeating. No one wants someone who appears desperate.

At one point, unable to find a Christian woman to go out with me, I started dating a nonbeliever. She seemed to be my fantasy-come-true! Blonde, blue-eyed, beautiful, popular. For a while we had fun, but I felt something was missing in the relationship. We couldn't share on a spiritual level, which was highly important to me. We could never be truly ONE. Heartsick, I broke off the relationship.

A Single Pastor

I graduated, entered the ministry, and was still single. I was teased unmercifully by almost everyone. Well-meaning Christians were always trying to introduce me to single Christian women. Everyone thought it was such a shame that I wasn't married!

I found it difficult at times to enjoy friendships with married people who wanted me to find someone so that I, too, would be a "normal" person. I discovered that singles tend to be forced into their own little isolated groups in order to survive. However, during these painful years of my life, God used the struggle to reveal to me an important truth: *Singleness is a part of God's plan!* The Bible says that in every situation God is working for the good of each believer (Romans 8:28). God is working in the situation of singleness, too!

Almost daily I committed my singleness to God, asking Him to show me what I was to gain from this experience. And He did.

But often, being human, I would cry out in my loneliness, "God, haven't I been single long enough?" It was tough trying to be cheerful about being alone when a part of me still desperately wanted someone to love and care for, someone who loved and cared for me. Once in a while I'd try to discuss the issue with God, reminding Him how much more effective I'd be in the ministry if I had a wife who could help me. I experienced times of anger, frustration, and even depression as I struggled to become satisfied as a single pastor.

Satisfied

The more committed I became to God, the more I resisted the temptation to give in to my longings for a mate, and the more I learned about the principles of keeping my thought life disciplined. I acknowledged that not accepting God's plan for my life right then was sin.

Overcoming wrong thoughts is no easy task. But Christians can never expect to have Christ-centered relationships unless there is victory over this temptation. To break the control of an improper thought life requires diligence and courage. Surely God wants us to live victorious lives! "For God did not give us a spirit of timidity, but a spirit of power, of love and of self-discipline" (2 Timothy 1:7). The key is to tap the power of God reigning within us and allow Him to cleanse us. Here are some steps to follow to control your thought life:

Admit your sin

To successfully experience the changing power of God you must see your wrong thoughts as God sees them—*sin.* First John 1:8,9 says, "If we claim to be without sin, we deceive ourselves and the truth is not in us. If we confess our sins, he is faithful and just and will forgive us our sins and purify us from all unrighteousness." This Scripture verse says that if we confess our sin He can cleanse us from ALL unrighteousness. Not a part of it, but all of it. As you're honest about your condition, the Holy Spirit will immediately begin to do the necessary housecleaning.

Desire a complete change

You must so want to be changed that you are willing to take the necessary steps to realize that change. It may mean giving more time to your devotional life, studying greater portions of God's Word, fasting. Any bondage or struggle can be overcome if you desire to tap God's strength. "Draw near to God and He will draw near to you" (James 4:8, NASB). As you do, He will replace your desires with His own. There, victory is found.

Share with someone close to you

Probably the most difficult struggle is the one that is faced alone. James 5:16 exhorts believers to confess their sins to other believers for support and prayer. Do not be foolish enough to share with everyone, of course, publicizing your struggles for the whole world. Enlist the support of one or two intimate Christian friends: their prayers, encouragement, and rebuke, if necessary. Struggles are not as bad when they are shared with spiritual confidants (see Galatians 6:1,2).

Use self-control

Although the power of God is working righteousness in us, we are free moral agents who must make choices. God can set you free, but if you continue to subject yourself to temptation that can overwhelm you, then the battle will rage on. Eliminate from your life those experiences, relationships, or reading materials that aggravate the problem. "Clothe yourselves with the Lord Jesus Christ, and do not think about how to gratify the desires of your sinful nature" (Romans 13:14). Choose your activities wisely. Paul did not deny the Corinthians' catchword "everything is permissible for me." He did point out, however, "not everything is beneficial. I will not be mastered by anything" (1 Corinthians 6:12). In other words, Paul chose to stay on the path of freedom by sowing to the Spirit, not the flesh. He could then expect the fruit of the Spirit to take root in his life, which includes self-control (translated "temperance" in the King James Version, Galatians 5:23).

Taking these four steps will put you on a path out of an undisciplined thought life. No longer conforming to the pattern of this world, you will be undergoing a transformation as you renew your mind with God's Word and counsel (see Romans 12:2). Of course, you will never be home free; temptation and testing is a part of the Christian experience. But you won't be the easy target for the enemy that you once were.

The difference between being overwhelmed by temptation and having victory over it lies in our desire to be like Jesus and serve Him always.

Bringing your thought life under control also opens the door to successful fellowship with the opposite sex. Putting aside selfish motives allows the two of you to grow in Christ together. When temptation does come, your commitment to one another in Jesus allows you to have victory.

And so, after much discipline and prayer I was able to pray, like Jesus, "Not my will, Father, but Yours." Most of the time I could add confidently and honestly "even if it means remaining single the rest of my life!"

Except that didn't happen. Instead I met Rebecca!

4

Becoming a Contented Single Woman

by Rebecca Larson

It is not always easy to be a single Christian woman. How well I know that!

Like many girls, I grew up planning to get married—*soon*. Most of us thought that something was wrong with us if we didn't have a steady boyfriend, or a husband, after we got out of high school. The threat of being an old maid loomed over our heads and clouded our judgment. We didn't realize that jumping into a hasty relationship could result in frustration, pain, and a wounded spirit. It was a long time before I learned that God is in control, and wants us to have a contented, abundant life—single or married!

Because I thought dating was the yellow brick road to happiness, I started dating quite young. All through junior and senior high school, I had steady boyfriends. The worst possible experience at that time was to spend a Friday or Saturday evening at home, without a date. So, I always made sure I had dates lined up for the weekends. I never really knew what it meant to be lonely or rejected. I was sure I would be married right on schedule.

A New Goal

Then during my last year in high school I accepted Jesus Christ as my Lord and Saviour. Now I had two life goals: to get married and to be in God's service. Deep in my heart was born a sincere desire to become a pastor's wife; so when God led me to go to a school of theology, I felt confident that He was preparing me for the ministry.

Yet, in spite of that confidence, I was struggling to discover where I fit in the body of Christ as a single woman. I was often frustrated and afraid as I wondered, *What can a single woman do for the Lord? Is there a place of effective ministry for me? Just what is God's purpose for my life?*

I sought counsel from spiritual advisors, but the answers were always the same: sing in the choir, play the piano, work in the nursery, teach Sunday school, or become a missionary. Even though I prayerfully considered these alternatives, I did not feel God's call to any of these ministries. Finally, I became convinced that without a man, I could never have a successful ministry.

It is truly tragic that many single women mistakenly feel that they are destined to be unfruitful in the Lord's work because they do not have a husband. Consequently, they sit back and wait for "Mr. Right" before they enter into ministry.

Feeling that way myself, I decided that God's purpose in bringing me to school was not only to study the Bible, but to find a Christian husband! And although I enjoyed studying and preparing for the Lord's service, I was more excited about meeting the man with whom I would spend the rest of my life. I used to daydream about what it would be like when we met: running through grassy fields hand in hand, times of laughing together, marching down the aisle in a white lace gown, a romantic honeymoon on a Pacific island, raising children, serving the Lord. What a beautiful dream! It was constantly on my mind as I developed an overpowering preoccupation with getting married.

During my classes I started checking out the boys, choosing which ones I wanted to meet based on my idea of a prospective husband. I'd think, *Ooo-hmmm—that one is good looking—better talk with him right after class!* And I would. I never told anyone these thoughts, and I doubt if anyone ever would have guessed how I felt. I wasn't a big flirt, just a marriage-struck girl, serious about reaching my goal.

The inevitable happened. Within a few months I met a young man who appeared to be everything I wanted in a husband. Overnight we became serious about our relationship and began hugging, kissing, and discussing marriage. It was wonderful!

Then one day his attitude changed, and he gave me the "brother-sister copout." That is the quick exit for someone who realizes the relationship has grown too intimate without God's blessing. A typical phrasing is, "I always thought of you as just a sister in the Lord. I never wanted our relationship to develop into anything more serious than friendship. I'll always love you as a sister."

What a blow! There I sat with my broken dreams. After sharing my life, my hopes and fears with this guy, he had just casually walked away! All along, deep inside, I had known that something was wrong with our relationship. Both our communication and emotional commitment had been superficial. Still, it hurt to lose the relationship. Being rejected is always painful.

Depression and Hope

I should have learned from that first experience, but I didn't. I went through a series of similar relationships.

This was new to me. After what I considered fruitful relationships as I was growing up, my college experience was full of loneliness and rejection. I began to believe I could never trust another man.

This was a difficult time in my life; my "season of singleness" seemed an eternity. What was God trying to teach me? I thought my emotional emptiness could be filled only by a man. And since I couldn't find "Mr. Right," there had to be something terribly wrong with me. Depression settled in. Often driving home from work, I would see couples in the other cars laughing and talking together. As loneliness would surge through me, I would weep, and cry out to God, "Why me, Lord? What's wrong with me?"

Becoming convinced that I was the ugliest girl in the world, I developed a poor self-image. Satan preyed upon my condition, trying to draw me away from God. Several non-Christian men who were interested in me, and who *appeared* to meet all of my needs, came into my life. I might have married any one of these men had I not recognized that it was Satan who was trying to tempt me. As hard as it was not to compromise my principles, I resisted this temptation through the power of God.

At this point I realized that God was trying to teach me a very important truth. He wanted to fill that void inside my heart. No human being can truly love us enough, satisfy our longings, or permanently take away our loneliness. Only God can fill that emptiness.

As He fills our beings, and we delight in Him, the desires of His heart become the desires of our heart. Then we understand David when he wrote, "Delight thyself . . . in the Lord; and he shall give thee the desires of thine heart. Commit thy way unto the Lord; trust also in him; and he shall bring it to pass" (Psalm 37:4,5, KJV).

We are so in tune with God that we no longer, among other things, "ask amiss" in our prayers (see James 4:3).

Attacked

I was trying wholeheartedly to make Jesus Christ Lord of this area of my life when I was shaken by a life-changing incident. While visiting friends, I was attacked by a vicious German shepherd. Before my friends were able to pull him off me, he had torn open my face, neck, and hands. I was certain the dog had bitten my jugular vein and I was going to bleed to death. As they rushed me to the hospital I was terrified, convinced I was dying.

In the emergency room I sobbed within myself, *Why has God allowed this?* I'll never forget what one orderly blurted out as he gazed at me, wide-eyed: "Oooh! Look at her face!" I burst out crying hysterically. Now I really was ugly! It took several orderlies to hold me down while the doctor cleaned and stitched the wounds. As he wrapped my face, the doctor tried to reassure me with the prospect of plastic surgery if the scars were too noticeable. Somehow, his words didn't comfort me!

At home I once again succumbed to dark depression. Here I was serving the Lord and this terrible experience happened. I pleaded with God to miraculously heal me. But the more I prayed, the more infected the wounds became. Soon, the right side of my face became abscessed and the stitches ripped open. I began to seriously doubt God's love for me; in bitterness I refused to see anyone. I refused to accept the possibility that I would be single *and* scarred *and* ugly all my life. During a tantrum one night, hurling pillows, papers, and books around my apartment, I even cursed God.

That same night I stubbornly refused to go to bed until God spoke to me. For hours I shouted at Him, demanding and pleading that He answer me. Finally, about 3:30 a.m., I broke down before God, asking forgiveness for my attitude. Promising to serve Him even if it meant being single and scarred, I repented. And God not only spoke to me in love, He touched me, healing me on the inside. At peace with God and myself, I slept.

The next day I called my pastor and told him of my change of heart. He immediately came over and took me to a Christian doctor, who was also a friend. Before beginning treatment, they both laid hands on me and asked God for physical healing. God answered their prayers. The abscesses disappeared and the skin healed. It was a miracle!

When I went back to the hospital for my scheduled check ups, the doctors and nurses couldn't believe that my face had healed so quickly. They rationalized the miracle by concluding that my skin was a special type that healed quickly. I knew better than that. I also knew that a more important healing had just as surely taken place: the healing of my spirit. I had never felt so close to God.

Remembering my promise, I sought to learn how to be completely happy as a single woman. It wasn't always easy. During those months I kept a notebook in which I wrote my prayers of loneliness and commitment. The notebook soon filled. Sometimes I was afraid. Sometimes I vacillated between fear and faith. One day I'd be crying out to God, "Why haven't you given me a husband yet? Why are you punishing me? I'm lonely, Lord!" Then a few days later I'd plead, "Oh, Lord, I want to be happy as a single woman. Help me to be willing to be single, if that is Your will for me."

Here are a few excerpts from my notebook.

Prayers From My Heart

Dear Jesus:

My heart is aching inside with a deep loneliness. I want You to help me overcome the pain, but the words won't come out right. How I long to be loved by someone! Help me to seek Your kingdom first, and to believe that You will add everything else I need to my life. Help me to trust You and Your timing. Once again I'm giving my life completely over to You; help me to leave it in Your hands instead of taking it back again like I often do. I'm tired of trying to work things out on my own. Help me to be happy as a single woman. Please!

Love,

Rebecca

Dear Jesus:

Why am I the way I am? Why do I let my imagination run wild? Why can't I hear Your voice clearly? Why can't I accept myself the way I am—a single woman? Lord, I want to be happy with just You as my *only* love. All I really want is to be in Your will, no matter what the cost *even if it means being single the rest of my life.* I pray that You take this rejection and hurt within my heart, and turn it into something beautiful. I turn over to You my desires for a husband. Lord, please help me to keep You first in my life.

Love,

Rebecca

Dear Father:

Have I been fulfilling Your purpose for my life? I hope so, because my greatest desire is to be in the center of Your will. You are the only true happiness.

As I look back over this year I realize how often I've felt sorry for myself. Sometimes I've wondered if my heart was made of stone or if I could ever love again. Thank you for allowing me to go through these experiences and to see Your purpose in them. Use me for Your glory.

I'm tired of living for myself. Show me where You want me and what You want me to do. Help me to do Your will.

Thank You for molding me into a godly woman through these trials. Let me be in Your ministry so that I can give glory and honor to You. Use me today, as a single woman!

I love You, Lord,

Rebecca

I gradually learned the most important lesson in my life. I can honestly say that I became a contented, happy single woman. I could never have done it without the Lord, or without daily surrendering my life to Him. He gave me the insight into what I had to do to become content. Some of the things I learned are shared in the next several chapters of this book: accepting myself, growing in the Lord, fellowshipping equally with all of my Christian brothers, and letting God supply all of my needs.

It wasn't God's plan for me to remain single all of my life; only that I learn to be content in His will. So, one day He brought Ray Larson into my life.

5
A Season of Singleness

Ecclesiastes 3 tells us that God governs man's activities, giving each of them a "season." Singleness also has a season. Most of us are not called to live all our lives unmarried, only a portion. Most of us experience a *season* of singleness, a time when we may learn important lessons about serving Him, and relating to others. The length, the timing, and the number of these seasons vary from person to person.

As a Christian you must not look upon singleness as a void, having nothing to offer you. Accept your single days and years, watching for the unique opportunity for growth they offer you. Without question, God is working in every situation to bring about total wholeness in your life. He can transform your single life into a prosperous and exciting spiritual adventure!

Purposes for the Season of Singleness

The season of singleness in our lives as Christians is ordained by God to teach us some important truths that will equip us for life, ministry, and possibly marriage. Let's examine two specific purposes for singleness:

It helps establish Jesus Christ as our first love

God has created us to enjoy a love relationship with

Him through His Son, Jesus Christ. Consequently, He wants us to love and enjoy His fellowship more than we cherish any human relationships. God wants to be our *first love.* "Love the Lord your God with all your heart and with all your soul and with all your mind and with all your strength" (Mark 12:30).

Our Heavenly Father desires every aspect of our lives to be characterized by a deep love and commitment to Jesus Christ. How often do we give first place to girl friends, boyfriends, husbands, and wives rather than to serving God? Yet Jesus said, "Anyone who loves his father or mother more than me is not worthy of me; anyone who loves his son or daughter more than me is not worthy of me" (Matthew 10:37).

This Scripture verse clearly teaches that Jesus must be the number one focus of our lives. We know something is amiss when we allow any human relationship to become more important than our relationship with Him. As we learn to love Jesus more and allow Him to reign, we can enjoy with other brothers and sisters meaningful relationships that have their rightful place in God's purposes for our lives. In fact, it is through our love for Jesus that we learn to love others!

A season of singleness helps to develop Christlike character for the fulfillment of His will

God knew each of us before we were born. The Psalmist said, "When my bones were being . . . carefully put together in my mother's womb, . . . you knew that I was there—you saw me before I was born" (Psalm 139:15, *Good News Bible*). And His purpose for our lives revolves around our conforming to the likeness of Jesus. Read Romans 8:29.

There are certain lessons we must learn for ministry

in the body of Christ that are best learned while single. For example, Rebecca, by nature a reserved person, developed an outgoing confidence during her years as a single adult. She also accepted the call to start a fellowship of students and, in having the time to give to that ministry, she developed excellent leadership traits.

A season of singleness is an excellent time for giving God our undivided attention, for allowing Him to mold us uniquely after His image.

Practical Aspects of the Season of Singleness

You might be thinking, *Those are noble ideals, but how do I make them work for me, and right now?* First, stop worrying about being single. Then begin to use, rather than merely bide, your time, taking advantage of the practical opportunities your single life-style affords.

Get to know God better

In 1 Corinthians 7:32-35, Paul wrote:

> I would like you to be free from concern. An unmarried man is concerned about the Lord's affairs—how he can please the Lord. But a married man is concerned about the affairs of this world—how he can please his wife—and his interests are divided. An unmarried woman or virgin is concerned about the Lord's affairs: Her aim is to be devoted to the Lord in both body and spirit. But a married woman is concerned about the affairs of this world—how she can please her husband. I am saying this for your own good, not to restrict you, but that you may live in a right way in undivided devotion to the Lord.

Although Paul wrote this to the Corinthian believers during a critical period (see vv. 26,29; *cf.* Ephesians 5:15,16), his observations about marriage hold whether or not our times are correspondingly critical.

Having less responsibility for the needs of an immediate family, singles find their time is freed to become intimate with the Lord. Invest more time reading God's Word. Develop your prayer life. Our society is geared toward keeping people physically active. Jesus' example, however, points to the need for diligent spiritual activity. Learning to spend time with God in solitude while single establishes a pattern that can strengthen your life and ministry.

Get involved in ministry for the Kingdom

Rather than moping around in loneliness, use your energies to meet someone's needs. We are commanded to "do nothing out of selfish ambition or vain conceit, but in humility consider others better than yourselves. Each of you should look not only to your own interests, but also to the interests of others" (Philippians 2:3,4). Many people are far lonelier than you. Investing your time in caring for others leaves little time for worrying about your own situation. You can be available to counsel whenever needed; comfort other members of the body of Christ or go into the streets to reach our hurting world. Single Christians can be an effective task force for the kingdom of God. You will be surprised how much joy and fulfillment you can find by getting involved in ministry.

You don't have to sit around and wait until you are married before you can serve the Lord. God uses single people. Our Lord was single. So, consider the needs in your church or community and use your time, talents, energies, and financial resources for His work.

Develop a positive self-image

Carefully assess your strengths and weaknesses and

accept yourself as one of God's unique creations. Acknowledge those characteristics and qualities that you like about yourself. Consider those areas you would like to change. Set goals and timetables for those changes, and start growing instead of wasting time comparing yourself unfavorably with others.

Remember to measure yourself by the character of Christ. We were predestined to be conformed to His image, not to that of others. Besides, it is inner beauty which pleases the Lord. First Samuel 16:7 tells us that "the Lord does not look at the things man looks at. Man looks at the outward appearance, but the Lord looks at the heart." And Proverbs 31:30 reminds us "charm is deceptive, and beauty is fleeting; but a woman who fears the Lord is to be praised."

So, work on developing inner beauty and affirm your progress. Allow God to make you into a special and unique person. There's no one in all the world just like you!

Learn to care and share through fellowship with other believers

By developing friendships with many brothers and sisters you can gain the kinds of relational skills you'll need even in marriage. Communicating clearly, cooperating on projects, creatively resolving conflicts, developing intimacy, forgiving and loving are skills that take time and practice to develop.

Through fellowship we can learn the true meaning of serving someone else. Jesus said, "Whoever wants to become great among you must be your servant, and whoever wants to be first must be your slave—just as the Son of Man did not come to be served, but to serve, and to give his life as a ransom for many" (Matthew 20:26-28).

Don't Waste The Opportunity

Being single allows you a great deal of personal freedom to make decisions and explore opportunities without adversely affecting the lives of others. For example, you can take a second job for a short while in order to save for a big purchase. You can give your full attention to work or school if needed. You can move, travel, or take up a hobby without consulting anyone else. Consider what things you want to experience in life and do them now. Then you won't look back at these years and regret missed opportunities.

What If I Never Marry?

Of course, a *life* of singleness is a possibility. Unfortunately many young Christians look upon this possibility with horror. If that is one's attitude, he certainly has not been "gifted" for it—for that is what singleness requires, an enablement from God.

Paul made this observation in the course of counseling the Corinthian Christians about marriage: "I wish that all men were as I am. But each man has his own gift from God; one has this gift, another has that" (1 Corinthians 7:7).

Paul was simply embodying what Jesus had taught: Some have "renounced marriage because of the kingdom of heaven" (Matthew 19:12). However, Paul recognized his celibacy was not achieved in his own strength. He spoke of it as a "gift from God," using the same Greek word for "gift" that he used in referring to the gifts of the Spirit in 1 Corinthians 12.

Singleness is not self-conferred; neither is it conferred by one's culture or peers or church—it is conferred by God, who enables the recipient to live it out. That "living it out" may be for a brief period, a lengthy period, or a lifetime. It may occur during young adulthood, during mid-life, or during one's final years.

So, how can you develop the right attitude about the single life-style and accept it joyfully? First, begin to enlarge your faith by thanking God for putting you into the situation that is best for your life. Second, commit yourself to do anything God asks of you. When you accept God's will, His peace will rule in your heart (see Philippians 4:6,7). Third, live one day at a time. *Today* God has called you to live and serve Him in singleness. As Jesus advised, let tomorrow take care of itself.

6
Fulfilled in Him

So often, for all of our talk about being whole persons, we still sense something lacking in our lives unless we have a loving relationship with a person of the opposite sex. We often hear a spouse spoken of as one's better *half*. Although much can be said for the fulfillment one finds in an intimate relationship, Paul has something more to say to us: "In Christ all the fullness of the Deity lives in bodily form, and you have this fullness in Christ" (Colossians 2:9).

Arguing against the notion that Christ was only one in a chain of deities, Paul adamantly stated that *all* the divine essence was in Christ.[1] More than that, Christ shares that fullness with believers; literally, wrote Paul, "you are fulfilled in Him."[2] Paul, of course, had in mind the spiritual adequacy of Christ's atoning work (see vv. 11-15) in contrast to the trickle-down theory of divinity promoted by certain teachers among the believers at Colossae: God at the top through numerous intermediaries to a few human beings in the know.

To say, however, that a person needs a spouse to be complete is to overlook the far-reaching effects of finding life in Christ.

Fulfilled?

One morning as Roberta was prayerfully meditating

during her quiet time, she visualized the Lord Jesus standing before her. Although she was usually comfortable with being single, that morning she was feeling somewhat sad and lonely. "Oh Lord," she prayed, "I've grown up through my experiences with relationships. I've learned so much. For what? I have so much love to give, but no one seems to want my love!"

Roberta, the Lord said gently, *give it to me! I want your love.*

Our relationship with the Lord can be the most intimate interaction imaginable. Who else knows our thoughts, accurately discerns our motives, listens forgivingly to our confessions of failures, and loves us forever? Ephesians 1:6 says we are "accepted in the beloved." No earthly mate can offer such complete acceptance and affirmation! *You are fulfilled in Him.*

The Lord Is My Friend and Companion

What about the idea of the Lord as our friend, our intimate, our confidant? Scripture talks about believers as being His friends (Proverbs 18:24; Luke 12:4; John 11:11; 15:15). How might we personalize this concept? Laurie, one of our single friends, shared her ideas from which we have drawn the following thoughts.

What does it mean to be an intimate friend of the Lord? Probably you can best understand if you think of how you would relate to a human friend in an ideal relationship.

You would in some way express affection and appreciation

"Loving is doing" is a phrase which summarizes the scriptural concepts of real love. John says, "Dear children, let us not love with words or tongue but with actions and in truth" (1 John 3:18). "The heavens declare the glory of God; the skies proclaim the work of his hands" (Psalm 19:1). When was the last time you noticed God's handiwork? How do you tell the Lord that you love Him?

You would communicate with your friend

Do you start your day by sharing with the Lord, or do you take time only to shower, dress, and gulp a cup of coffee? Begin to incorporate early morning communion with God into your routine, and your days will be anything but routine! You might start by praying as you jog (or exercise) and praising as you shower. Real joy comes, however, when you actually set aside some quality time to just fellowship with the Lord.

You would give priority to your friend

Your commitment to an intimate will be high on your list of loyalties. How much more so in a relationship with the Lord Jesus Christ! He is to have preeminence in our lives. And when our priorities are in order, God adds to our lives those things we need in order to live the abundant life (see Matthew 6:33; John 10:10; Philippians 4:19).

You would be proud of your friend and your relationship

When you love someone, you are proud to introduce that person to anyone and tell about the special relationship you have.

Laurie writes, "Lord, let me be that proud of You! Let me be eager to introduce You to those I meet, as I would be eager to introduce my love to them. I want people to realize how lucky I am to have You loving me . . . how fortunate I am that You have chosen *me* to be Your bride. Thank You, Lord, that You walk with me, protecting me . . . that I can 'beam' as others do when they are with someone they love."

Can people tell by looking at you that you are in love with the Lord? Are you proud of your relationship and eager to introduce people to God? Or, is your relationship as secret as that of a spouse who refuses to wear a wedding ring?

You would respect your friend's judgments and wishes

When you genuinely love someone, you value that person's ideas and opinions. Sometimes, however, we have trouble trusting the Lord's judgments. Often we aren't sure that what God has in mind for us is what *we want*! But consider God's encouragement of the exiled Israelites: "I know the plans I have for you . . . plans to prosper you and not to harm you, plans to give you hope and a future" (Jeremiah 29:11).

God wants only our highest good, and since only He can look into the future, only He knows what will work out for us. Consider Joseph's "reunion address" to his brothers, making an assessment of everything that happened to him (being sold into slavery by his brothers, imprisoned by Potiphar, forgotten by the chief cupbearer): "You intended to harm me, but God intended it for good" (Genesis 50:20).

You would share what you have

Sharing is one of the first things parents try to teach their children. Friendships are more easily made if we have learned to share. Probably our greatest treasure, which we have equally and want to keep for ourselves, is time.

You would be loyal to your friend

We face so many temptations each day that can lure us into sin. But "no temptation has seized you except what is common to man. And God is faithful; he will not let you be tempted beyond what you can bear. But when you are tempted, he will also provide a way out so that you can stand up under it" (1 Corinthians 10:13).

And yet, sometimes we fail to use the escape hatch the Lord has provided, and instead we follow the paths of sin, only to discover separation, sorrow, and frustration. But praise the Lord for the promise of forgiveness if we will turn and confess our sins to Him (1 John 1:9).

The Lord as a Friend

Let's see how the Lord responds in each of the above areas.

He loves us

Not only did He love us enough to die for us (Romans 5:8) but He did it willingly (John 10:17,18). His Word is full of "I love you" messages. And His daily miracles remind us that we are loved.

He is the Jehovah-Jireh of the Old Testament—our Provider! Every need is met: physical, emotional, spiritual (Philippians 4:19). And even our desires are granted when we put God first in our lives (Psalm 37:4,5). He protects us, guides us, cares for us, watches over us, and underneath us "are the everlasting arms" (Deuteronomy 33:27).

Jesus Christ went back to heaven to prepare a place for us so that where He is, we may be also (John 14:1-3). His entire message has been one of eternity. Eternal love. Together forever.

He communicates with us

God has given us the most significant of communications—the Bible. Among other things it is autobiographical. For example, in John 16:12-15 He is saying, "This is who I am and how I act. This is everything I want to tell you. And, if you have any problems with understanding my Word, the Holy Spirit will explain it."

He gives us priority consideration

Not only does He hear our prayers, but in Jeremiah 33:3 God says, "Call to me and I will answer you and tell you great and unsearchable things you do not know." In Isaiah 65:24 we are told "Before they call I will answer; while they are still speaking I will hear."

He wants to be proud of us

In Ephesians 5:25-27 Paul tells us that Christ loved the Church and gave His life for us so that He could present us to himself as His radiant and pure bride. Christ sees us for what we will become. He has begun a good work in us, and will continue it until that day when He can introduce us to the Father (Philippians 1:6).

He respects our will, our feelings

Look at the honesty embodied in the psalms (especially 22, 31, 39, 42, 88, and 142). Consider Moses' reluctance to accept God's call to lead the Hebrew people (see Exodus 3:11 to 4:13). Witness Job's expressions of perplexity to God (e.g., 7:11-21 and 9:17-24), Ecclesiastes' despair (1:2-11ff.), Peter's presumptuousness (e.g., Mark 14:27-31).

A human spouse can read only written letters, or hear

only spoken words. But the Lord reads our thoughts and probes our hearts. He knows our motives and nothing is hidden from Him. And yet, He urges us to come boldly unto the throne of grace *to find help in time of need!* (Hebrews 4:12-16). "For the one who knows us best loves us most."[3]

He shares with us

Jesus shared himself with His disciples. "Peace I leave with you: my peace I give you" (John 14:27). He also gave them His joy (see John 15:11)—and finally His life. As His disciples, we receive the same from Him.

He is faithful

"I will be with you always, to the very end of the age" (Matthew 28:20). We need never worry that He no longer loves us. He has made an eternal commitment to us.

It's Not the Same!

There is an obvious difference in having a human friend and relating to the Lord as your friend. He is not available to our five senses. We hear no voice, see no smile, feel no hug. But physical involvement is not the heart of a relationship, it is only one expression of love.

A relationship is an emotionally intimate commitment. And in that sense, we can find all we need in the Lord.

We can be fulfilled in Him!

---

[1] Ralph Martin, *Colossians and Philemon* (Greenwood, SC: Attic Press, 1974), p. 80.

[2] D. Guthrie and J. A. Mortyer, eds., *The New Bible Commentary: Revised* (Grand Rapids, MI: Wm. B. Eerdmans Pub. Co., 1970), p. 1147.

[3] Bill Gaither, "I Am Loved," © 1978 by the Gaither Music Company, Alexandria, IN.

7

Are You Ready for Company?

Henry had come to me for counseling. He said he was ready to get married, but he wasn't sure what to do next. As he talked, I noticed that Henry's hair looked as though it had not been washed in over a week, his shirt was spotted and wrinkled, and his pants were quite dirty. Taking a cue from his personal appearance, I began asking about other areas of his life.

I discovered that Henry did not read the Word or pray on a daily basis. His checkbook was unbalanced, and his account overdrawn. In virtually every area I inquired about, Henry lacked discipline! I thought, *Brother, do you think God is going to lead a girl into this mess?*

As we talked, Henry began to realize the need for a few changes in his life. "I guess I'd better clean up my mess!" he laughed, a little sheepishly. And with a lot of encouragement and a little help from his pastor and friends, Henry did just that!

When Guests Are Coming

When we know that guests are coming to our homes, we usually do some extra housecleaning. But when it comes to waiting for a mate to come along and share our lives, we don't always keep up with our personal housekeeping! How can we expect to be successful in a lifelong caring relationship with another person if we haven't learned how to take care of ourselves?

Key areas in which single adults need to check their housekeeping skills include home cleanliness, personal responsibilities, finances, family life, personal hygiene and appearance, and spiritual growth. *If you have major problems in any of these areas, you aren't ready for marriage!* Marriage is a sharing relationship. How can God's wonderful, ideal plan for someone else's life be to share your life if what you have to offer is one big mess? "God is not a God of disorder, but of peace" (1 Corinthians 14:33). Chaos does not reflect the work of God.

This is not to say that we must be perfect before we can expect to be married, for none of us will ever attain perfection in this life. However, that is no excuse for not taking charge of our lives, "for God did not give us a spirit of timidity, but a spirit of power, of love and of self-discipline" (2 Timothy 1:7).

It seems many singles believe that besides covering a multitude of sins, love overlooks laziness, sloppiness, uncleanliness, and irresponsibility. They think that when the right person comes along, everything in their own lives will suddenly fall into place, as if by magic. Not true! Personal housekeeping just like acutal housecleaning involves a lot of hard work and constant attention. And while it is true that when we are in love with someone we seem to have an incredible tolerance for that person's weaknesses, it is also true that the day-to-day intimacy of a marriage relationship can magnify even small irritations into intolerable problems. So, the more personal discipline you achieve, the better prepared you are to share your life with the person you love.

Marriage Is . . .

Marriage is a beautiful relationship, but it is not the

fantasy that childhood fairy tales and romantic television movies would have us believe. Knights in shining armor on white horses and lovely princesses do not live happily ever after when they say "I do." (Maybe that's why the fairy tales end as soon as the couples get married!)

Neither is marriage the acquisition of someone to take care of us, either by providing for our financial needs, protecting us from the outside world, or providing maid services.

Sometimes the hardest lesson we have to learn as adults is that we have to learn to assume the responsibility of caring for ourselves. We are no longer children to be looked after by our parents. And we cannot sit around waiting for a spouse to come along and take over where our parents left off.

The real joy in a marriage is not in receiving, but in giving! In Acts 20:35, Luke quotes the Lord Jesus as saying that "it is more blessed to give than to receive" (KJV). Yet, too frequently our dreams of marriage lay all of the responsibility on the other person! A truly successful marriage is a union of two whole people, not of two halves leaning on one another for support and survival.

So, get out the mop, bucket, cleanser, and broom, and start your personal housekeeping right now!

One, Two, Three—Grow!

A positive aspect of a period of singleness is the time for personal housekeeping and putting your life in order. This is the time for individual evaluation and growth. As you discover areas in which you need to develop discipline, seek the help of the Holy Spirit in those areas. Strive to improve your life, not just to become attractive to, or prepared for, a potential mate, but to *please the Lord*. Take to heart Paul's prayer for the Colossians:

> Since the day we heard about you, we have not stopped praying for you and asking God to fill you with the knowledge of his will through all spiritual wisdom and understanding. And we pray this in order that you may live a life worthy of the Lord and may please him in every way: bearing fruit in every good work, growing in the knowledge of God, being strengthened with all power according to his glorious might so that you may have great endurance and patience, joyfully giving thanks to the Father, who has qualified you to share in the inheritance of the saints in the kingdom of light (Colossians 1:9-12).

How do you measure up in each of the following areas?

Spiritual Life

Every Christian needs a committed devotional life. A man cannot be the spiritual leader of a family if he is not spiritual himself. A woman cannot encourage her husband and family in spiritual growth if she is not developing her own relationship with Jesus Christ. The question is, How is your personal relationship with the Lord, and the body of believers? Do you

1. read the Word systematically for understanding and guidance? (John 15:1-14)
2. commune with the Lord, regularly, offering thanks and praise, making your requests known to Him? (1 Thessalonians 5:17, Philippians 4:6)
3. faithfully attend church? (Hebrews 10:25)
4. fellowship with the body of believers, caring and sharing together? (Galatians 6:2)
5. exercise your spiritual gifts? (Ephesians 4:7-14)
6. memorize Scripture? (Psalms 119:11)
7. have the fruit of the Spirit evident in your life: love,

joy, peace, patience, kindness, goodness, faithfulness, gentleness, and self-control? (Galatians 5:22,23)
8. live a forgiven life? (1 John 1:9-2:3)

Home Cleanliness

The way you keep your home is a reflection of your personal priorities. A messy room, house, or car may be communicating a sense of confusion, or laziness, to others. Furthermore, researchers tell us that clutter in one's surroundings often tends to raise a person's anxiety level, while order has a calming effect. If you are always "just too busy" to clean house, then you just may be *too busy*! Do you
1. have a regular schedule of housecleaning?
2. keep your home reasonably clutter-free?
3. maintain the home in good repair?
4. keep up your yard?
5. drive a clean car?

Personal Hygiene and Appearance

Although relationships involve the whole person, outward appearances are also important if we are to be attractive to others. If being friends with a slovenly person is uncomfortable, marrying such a person would be unbearable. Other factors, such as being overweight, out of shape, or lacking good manners, can also make the "package" unattractive.

If we as Christians truly accept the concept that our bodies are the temple of the Holy Spirit (1 Corinthians 6:19,20), we might become better keepers of His house. One church started a weekly exercise program for "temple toners." Do you
1. eat a well-balanced, sensible diet?

2. exercise regularly?
3. keep yourself clean and well-groomed?
4. dress modestly and attractively?
5. relax frequently?
6. get sufficient rest?
7. watch your health?
8. treat your body as the temple of the Holy Spirit?

Finances

Financial responsibility is often a problem for single adults. Although most of those having money problems cite inadequate incomes or resources as the cause, the real culprit is usually poor management of what they do have. Unnecessary purchases, keeping up with the Joneses, and over-extended credit can create financial nightmares.

One engaged couple was experiencing a great deal of conflict over finances. The woman had accumulated several hundred dollars in bills, which she was expecting her fiancé to pay. Obviously, he was not comfortable with the situation. She was indignant. After all, she reasoned, wasn't a husband supposed to be the provider?

Obviously she needed to learn financial responsibility before she would be ready for a cooperative marriage relationship.

How do you rate in this area? Do you

1. have and live within a reasonable budget?
2. resist impulse buying, unnecessary purchases, or things you cannot afford?
3. save regularly?
4. plan and save for large purchases or investments?
5. have adequate insurance (car, health, dental)?
6. keep your checkbook balanced?

7. honor God with your tithes and offerings? (1 Corinthians 16:1,2)
8. use extra money to help needy brothers and sisters in the Lord? (2 Corinthians 8:13-15; 9:10,11)

Personal Responsibility

One of the basics of a good relationship is trust. And trust is built by making and keeping commitments. To the extent that you are reliable and responsible, people will trust you. Failing to keep your word, breaking confidences, procrastinating, always being late, and not following through on plans and promises are ways of undermining people's trust in you.

If you want someone to trust you enough to want to spend the rest of his life with you, then you must demonstrate your trustworthiness in all of your other relationships: on the job, with friends, with your family, or in the church. If you are irresponsible in these relationships, how can a potential mate expect you to be responsible in a marriage relationship? Do you

1. accept responsibilities joyfully?
2. follow through with plans/promises on a timely basis?
3. take commitments seriously?
4. keep the confidences of others?
5. genuinely care about others?
6. maintain a servant attitude in your relationships?
7. find that people consider you a responsible adult?
8. trust others?

Family Life

What about your relationship with your family? If you have a family and live near them, do you have an active role in their lives? Our relationships with our parents and siblings are a good indicator of how we will relate to a spouse and children, for we tend to repeat familiar habit patterns. And if you have not developed a positive relationship with the family God has given you, how can you expect God to give you a new family with which to struggle? The same holds true of our relationships with the members of the family of God.

James says that often people bless God out of one side of their mouths, while cursing people out of the other side. Any believer should be able to recognize the inconsistency of his life if he behaves this way. A wise person relates to both God and others with purity, peaceableness, gentleness, approachability, mercy, goodness, equality, and honesty (James 3:8-18). What a challenge—both with your own family, and the family of God! How are you disposed toward them?

1. available?
2. interested?
3. loving?
4. giving?
5. forgiving?
6. gentle?
7. empathetic?
8. honest?
9. uncritical and accepting?
10. encouraging?
11. helpful?
12. serving?

We grow to maturity in many other areas but these are among the basic problem areas we find in counseling singles who want to be married.

If you have discovered some areas in which you need to grow, sit down and develop goals in those areas. Then write out a detailed plan to reach each goal you have set. Assign starting and completion dates to each step of your plans. And implement your plans. Finally, periodically review your progress and celebrate your successes. You are becoming conformed to the image of Christ.

Would You Date You?

The decisive question in this chapter on self-appraisal is Would you date you? Knowing yourself as well as you do, could you honestly say that you are everything you would look for in a date? If not, then you probably have some growing to do (along with the rest of us).

As we have pointed out, an advantage of a *season of singleness* is the opportunity to give God your undivided attention, somewhat the way Paul did immediately after his conversion (see Galatians 1:15-18). You can gain perspective, maturity, mellowness. Fortunately, we do not have to be perfect before we can be used of God, or get married. Actually, maturing is a life-long process. So start now—become the person God designed you to be!

8

Mending Relationships

According to many psychologists, our lives are the sum of our experiences. What a person is today is the result of his good and bad experiences, especially in relating to others. In his book *Hide or Seek*, Dr. James Dobson describes the wretched life of Lee Harvey Oswald to show what may very well have motivated him to shoot President Kennedy. Oswald's constantly being rejected developed within him abject feelings of inferiority and failure. President Kennedy represented just the opposite of what Oswald had become. The shocking crime Oswald carried out on November 22, 1963, was the sum of negative relationships in his life, so implies Dr. Dobson.

A Christian does not have to be a psychologist to understand how experiences within relationships develop one's outlook on life. Life at its very basic level is relationship—relationship with oneself, relationship with God, relationship with others. How we view these relationships will dictate the success we will have in living life itself. Our relationships with our parents will play a part in how we will respond to others—including any children we may have. Our relationships with siblings are models of future interactions with Christian brothers and sisters. Early friendships develop patterns that tend to be repeated in later years. And in the same way, our past dating relationships will affect our attitudes in future relationships with the opposite sex, including a spouse.

This might seem to say that we are prisoners of our past, that whatever happens to us determines the outcome of our lives. Not exactly. Although what Dr. Dobson says about the responses of others shaping our lives is true, a power exists that can enable us to overcome the past. That power is the Holy Spirit, as Dr. Dobson goes on to discuss. A Christian can make major mistakes in his/her relationships and still have a successful spiritual life. God's love can mend broken relationships and heal bad experiences, laying a proper foundation for successful future relationships. Given the opportunity, the Holy Spirit could have done a healing in Lee Harvey Oswald's life, so that he could have developed a sense of self-worth apart from the unsympathetic people around him. God is a God of miracles!

In view of experiences influencing attitudes, examine your past relationships with the opposite sex. What type of success have you had in your relationships? When you think of those relationships, are you reminded of individuals you helped draw closer to Jesus? If friendship, honesty, and spiritual growth characterized your past relationships, then you probably can expect that same pattern to continue in the future. On the other hand, if dishonesty, game playing, and selfishness characterized your relationships, then you have established a bad pattern that you might follow again.

Having an honest and loving relationship is difficult if past relationships have been dishonest and selfish. If you have been the victim of an unhealthy relationship or have caused such a relationship, you could repeat your mistakes unless the Holy Spirit is permitted to heal the wounds.

More importantly, if a wounded spirit exists, the bond

of unity between two believers is broken. The only outcome is bitterness, resentment, and disappointment. Often the bitterness will spread to others close to the relationship and create a division in the body of Christ. We have seen a broken relationship tear apart an entire fellowship. When a relationship is damaged, the people outside the relationship are frequently forced to take sides, potentially polarizing even the strongest grouping.

A further aspect of broken relationships is their cumulative effect. Don't bring leftover bitterness and hurt to new relationships or you might end up dumping the garbage from the past on the new person.

Symptoms of a Wounded Spirit

Solomon wrote, "A man's spirit sustains him in sickness, but a crushed spirit who can bear?" (Proverbs 18:14). "A cheerful heart is good medicine, but a crushed spirit dries up the bones" (Proverbs 17:22). Is your spirit wounded? Have you wounded one of your brothers or sisters in Christ? Here are some signals that may indicate a need for forgiveness, healing, and reconciliation.

Hindered Fellowship and Friendship

All relationships in the kingdom of God should draw people closer to Jesus and to one another. A dating relationship builds into an intimate friendship as the two people spend time together and invest in each other's lives. Therefore, even if the dating relationship is terminated, the friendship should remain. True, letting go of the romantic aspect of the relationship may require a period without mutual contact, but failure to remain friends usually signifies spirits that need healing.

Uneasiness

Another sign of a wounded spirit is your feeling uncomfortable when thinking about a person with whom you once had a relationship. You know in your heart that something went wrong if you cannot wish the best for that person. If your conscience is not clear when thinking about that relationship, you may find the Holy Spirit is trying to tell you everything is not well.

Negative Comments

Jesus denounced the Pharisees, saying, "Out of the overflow of the heart the mouth speaks" (Matthew 12:34). If in the course of a conversation the name of a person with whom you had a dating relationship is brought up, and you start saying negative things about that person, you probably have a wounded spirit. On the other hand, if you learn that that individual has been making negative comments about you, then you can assume that the other person feels wounded in spirit. Negative comments about a former friend are usually a sign of broken fellowship.

Fear of Risking

When people have wounded spirits, they often develop an abnormal fear of risking new relationships. They develop a wariness, a reluctance to trust again. If a new relationship does develop and then terminates, they tend to make comments like, "Well, I was rejected again," signifying that the new pain is being added to the former pain. Using the term "again" in these situations is usually an indication of a wounded spirit.

A relationship should be looked upon as a trust given to us by the other person. He has made himself vulnerable to the pain of caring. This is especially true of the relationship between a man and a woman. If this trust is damaged, we must act responsibly by seeking to restore understanding, if not fellowship. Ask God to show you any relationship you have that may need restoration.

Rebuilding the Bridges Behind You

Jesus said, "If you are offering your gift at the altar and there remember that your brother has something against you, leave your gift there in front of the altar. First go and be reconciled to your brother; then come and offer your gift" (Matthew 5:23,24).

In the Old Testament to present an offering at the altar was an act of worship. In these two verses, Jesus was saying that if in worship toward God a person recognized a problem in one of his relationships, he was directly to make things right with that person. Then return to worship God. In other words, our relationship to God is directly affected by how we treat one another.

As always, God's Word provides the answers to our problems. Because God knows that we will make mistakes, He has provided the method for us to grow through those mistakes. If you hurt another person, then your first step is to take the *responsibility* by acknowledging where you were wrong.

Next, go to that person, confess what you did wrong (be brief; there is no need to go into detail), and ask for forgiveness. As you humbly seek to restore your friendship, the Holy Spirit can bring healing and forgiveness. According to Scripture, that person should accept your apology and forgive you (Luke 17:1-4; Ephesians 4:32). Thus the Holy Spirit can restore unity to the body of Christ. The actual reestablishment of the friendship may take a little time because new roles will have to be developed (e.g., friend vs. dating partner), but the foundation will have been laid and the healing begun.

You may find, however, that the other person is not willing to forgive you because he is still deeply hurt, bitter, or resentful. Don't try to force that person to forgive you. Instead, acknowledge the pain which he is experiencing, and then continue to treat that person as you would a good friend. Prove that your repentance is genuine. Remember, God has forgiven you, and you are being obedient to the Word. Pray for that person, that the love of God will heal the wounded spirit.

If you are the wounded party, spend some time in prayer about your feelings. Tell the Father about the pain, and search your heart to see if you are harboring inappropriate anger, resentment, or vengefulness. Have you genuinely been wronged; or have you simply been rejected? Have you taken offense when none was meant? Has your spirit been wounded, or just your pride?

If you sincerely conclude that you have been wronged and honestly cannot resolve the matter within yourself (*cf.* 1 Peter 4:8; 1 Corinthians 13:4-7; and Matthew 6:14,15), then Matthew 18:15-17 gives the steps you need to take to restore the relationship: "If your brother sins against you, go and show him his fault, just between the two of you. If he listens to you, you have won your brother over. But if he will not listen, take one or two others along, so that 'every matter may be established by the testimony of two or three witnesses.' If he refuses to listen to them, tell it to the church; and if he refuses to listen even to the church, treat him as you would a pagan or a tax collector."

When you go to the one who has hurt you, be sure you go with love. Gently describe the action that hurt you. Explain your response to that action. Probably that person will ask your forgiveness. If you prayed about confronting this person, relying on the leading of the Holy Spirit for the timing and wording of your approach, seldom are the other steps of this Scripture needed; the other person's heart has usually been prepared by God to receive you.

Either way, whether you are the wrongdoer or the wronged, the Lord instructs you to take the initiative to be reconciled. We have no excuse for coming to worship the Lord without having attempted to resolve a difference between us and a believer.

"Before discovering correct principles for Christ-centered relationships," Don admits, "I blundered through a half-dozen encounters with my Christian sisters. The guilt and disappointment from each of my past experiences strongly affected my next relationship. Then God began to clearly show me my wrong motives and actions, and I began to make restitution with the sisters whose spirits had been wounded from the past. The guilt soon left. I began to see ways to effectively implement scriptural guidelines for relationships. Fellowship with the opposite sex began to work because I had a clean slate, a clear conscience, and good principles with which to share. The Lord brought some encouraging relationships into my life that taught me many important insights that later would significantly help me in marriage."

Don't Panic!

A common response to a presentation on forgiveness is panic, a desire to immediately dash out and clear up any misunderstandings before the day is over. Relax. Take time to discuss your feelings with God before going to others. The fact that you are willing to forgive and to seek forgiveness shows that your attitude is pleasing to God. Plan how to contact people in person or by telephone. Don't document and record your sins by writing a letter. Ask God to work out the opportunity for you to restore fellowship where needed.

On the other hand, when the Holy Spirit opens up an opportunity for reconciliation, don't pass it up.

Worship God

When you, with the help of the Holy Spirit, have restored the broken relationships from your past, Jesus says to come and offer your gift (worship) to God. You are now free to have a full relationship with God. You are free to grow spiritually. And since your relationship with God is linked to your relationships with others, you will want to treat present, and future, relationships with care.

Besides your present well-being, your future depends on the quality of your relationships. Don't ignore the broken relationship—mend it!

9
Caring and Sharing

After I addressed a singles group one evening, a very pretty girl came up to me and asked, "How do I go about becoming friends with this guy in our group? I mean, I don't want to be considered too forward. Besides, if God wanted us to be friends, wouldn't He give the guy the idea?"

You've probably had similar thoughts at one time or another. Such thoughts reflect a basic problem with boy-girl relationships in our culture. We regard relationships with persons of the opposite sex as having a purpose beyond mere friendship. A gesture of friendship toward a member of the opposite sex seems to imply an interest in that person as a dating partner or a potential mate. Such thinking creates an unnecessary tension between single men and women.

Love One Another

Jesus said, "A new command I give you: Love one another. As I have loved you, so you must love one another" (John 13:34). Jesus had friends of both sexes. He enjoyed the friendship of women, seeing them as spiritual sisters (see Mark 3:31-35). He cared how they felt, and shared with His friends during the sad times as well as in the good times. Remember Jesus' friendship with Mary, Martha, and Lazarus. And His commandment is that we love one another, the way He loved.

Are you willing to reach out to all of your Christian brothers and sisters in the love of the Lord? If you do, you will be amazed at the number of close friendships you will form, and how much love will flood back into your life.

General Fellowship

We need to get to know and establish friendships with the brothers and sisters in our local community of believers in order to have a full spiritual life. Sometimes it's tough to be just friends with a member of the opposite sex. If you are seen talking or sitting in church with someone more than once, you're likely to be asked if the two of you are going together. Or, if you go out to dinner a few times with someone, you're both labeled out of circulation. And if you engage in activities with a variety of friends of the opposite sex, you are often viewed as "afraid to make a commitment" or "immature, not ready to settle down." This ought not to be so.

The fellowship of believers should not be limited to friends of the same sex or potential mates. To do so would severely limit your choice of friends. There are many terrific people who would make wonderful friends, but to whom you would not choose to be married. Why deny yourself those wonderful friendships? And why deny your friendship to someone just because you don't want to marry that person?

Learn to approach all of your brothers and sisters in Christ as potential friends. Let people get to know you. Share yourself. Discover ways you can be of service to others. Use your spiritual gifts to minister. Love without expectations. Care in practical ways as well as in words (see 1 John 3:18). Discover people God wants you to reach out to, and do so. God sends many relationships into our lives to teach us spiritual truths. In fact, our friendships have a significant influence on our personal and spiritual growth. Developing new friendships through general fellowship offers you a chance for growth.

Certainly we were created sexual beings and we need not deny that, but we can interrelate with the opposite sex in ways that do not induce romance. In other words, when we say to "go out with" or spend time "fellowshipping" with all of your brothers and sisters, we are not implying a physical involvement. That commitment is reserved for an exclusive dating relationship with one member of the opposite sex, as we will discuss in the next chapter. Fellowshipping comprises only intellectual, social, and spiritual involvement in one another's lives.

How Does This Work?

No one should be excluded from fellowship. Yet, many people feel lonely and rejected because they often are overlooked for evenings of fellowship, and assume they do not possess the characteristics and qualities "required" for dating. Such loneliness is a burden many have been forced to carry because of our practice of fellowshipping with potential mates only. Physical beauty is not a valid requirement for friendship. "Besides," commented Walt, one of the men in our singles group, "after you get to know someone, you don't even notice what that person looks like." When superficial limitations are removed from our requirements for a friend, we are often surprised by the number of good friendships we develop.

While still single, I sought fellowship with a girl I would normally have overlooked. After just one evening of fellowship, I was dumbfounded. She was so much fun to be with! Her personality was delightful, her character strong and sweet. We became friends, and today she is one of my closest sisters. Through her friendship, I grew. Our time together eased our mutual struggle with loneliness. Yet, I almost missed the chance to get to know her.

Our society places much emphasis on having someone special in our lives, someone with whom we "belong." As brothers and sisters reach out to one another, they can help each other cope with that sense of being all alone. We need each other.

John invited many different sisters to fellowship for an evening. His goal was to develop new friendships, and to stop shopping for a spouse. One evening over dinner he shared a secret dream he'd had for years—to sing the national anthem at Angel Stadium in Anaheim, California. He stopped when he saw that his friend was smiling.

"I guess you think I'm silly," he said, almost wishing he hadn't said anything about his dream. "I don't ever expect to do it," he continued, "but I guess most singers have some such fantasy."

"Oh, no!" his friend hurried to explain, "I don't think you're silly. I was smiling because what you don't know is that one part of my job is to schedule people to sing 'The Star-Spangled Banner' at Angel Stadium!"

Two weeks later John stepped to the microphone and sang to a full stadium!

Of course, not every person you fellowship with will make your dreams come true. Maybe you are the one who is to be the giver. In either case, your general fellowship will fulfill two important responsibilities.

1. Unity in the Body.

Selective dating can bring factions to the body of believers, while general fellowship can result in a sense of harmony and unity.

2. Ministry to the lonely.

Being sensitive to people's needs, reaching out to the lonely, can help people escape their own loneliness. This is not to imply that you walk up to someone and say, "I'm going to fellowship with you as a ministry to the lonely!" But just be ready to care for and share with one another in times of need. Remember times when you have felt lonely? Wouldn't you have enjoyed some company? As you reach out and share you will be blessed in a new way.

Okay! So What Do I Do?

If you've decided to open your life to a new dimension in relationships, to developing friendships without expectations, you will need to take three steps.

Throw away your shopping list

Most of us have a list of characteristics and qualities which we want in a mate. As we meet members of the opposite sex, we tend to measure them against our mental list, and to turn away from those who don't match it. For general fellowship to work, you have to throw away the list. Remember, you're not shopping for a mate. You are just making friends. To value one person over another is to show favoritism, which is contrary to the command to love. "My brothers, as believers in our glorious Lord Jesus Christ, don't show favoritism" (James 2:1).

God doesn't exclude any of us from His fellowship. We are all equal before Him. And we must apply that same principle among the household of faith. How can we judge a person by such qualities as appearance and talent? We can't. That is the world's way. "The Lord does not look at the things man looks at. Man looks at the outward appearance, but the Lord looks at the heart" (1 Samuel 16:7). Ask God to help you see people as He does.

Reach out in fellowship

Invite different ones to dinner, to a concert, for a walk along the beach, for coffee, to a sports event. Talk, listen, share ideas, goals, and accomplishments. Be courteous, gentle, caring, and understanding. Don't get involved in suggestive comments, come-on looks, exploitive attitudes, and the games men and women often play when they are trying to impress each other.

Be yourself. Become a genuine friend people can trust. People won't get the wrong idea if you keep an attitude of friendship and camaraderie.

Following this exhortation to fellowship as members of God's family, many of the single adults in our church set aside old ways and began to reach out and share together. One man developed solid friendships with several Christian women. One day he expressed surprise at how much he was learning about being a Christian through the example of those women!

When you reach out to give friendship, be willing to receive in return. If you are going around investing in or fixing up other people's lives without allowing them to minister to you, you may soon feel empty and used. And you rob people of the joy of giving to you. Besides, the Bible says that God distributed spiritual gifts among the believers so they could minister to and build one another up (Ephesians 4:11-16).

As you reach out, you will probably be attracted to some people more than others. You will discover that you want to spend more time with some in order to know them better. Some will become close friends. Others will remain casual friends. A few will become your intimate friends. That's fine. But don't focus all of your time, energy, and attention on just a few intimate friendships or the result will be small cliques. Divide your attention appropriately so that you have time to meet new people and develop new friendships. Reaching out is an ongoing responsibility because there are always new people to meet and get to know.

Clarify your objective

The best way to maintain a spirit of fellowship with a member of the opposite sex is to share your motives. *A lot is assumed from silence.* In the beginning, and in the course of your fellowship with someone, communicate your desire to keep the relationship on a brother/sister level so no one can doubt your motives.

Many of Rebecca's best friends are Christian brothers. They went out to dinner, studied together, and shared needs with one another during their college days. Open communication between them kept their relationship in perspective. Thus, when I came into Rebecca's life, those brothers became my friends as well, and we all spent time together. They did not show resentment—they accepted me as her choice for a romantic relationship.

As you reach out, keep your communication lines clear. Discuss the objectives for the friendship with one another. It's possible that your motives might change for a particular friendship once you get to know someone well. You may decide that you want a closer, or even a romantic, relationship with that person. Relax. If you have turned your future over to God and are in close fellowship with Him, He will lead you in the direction you should go. God doesn't have a communication problem. He won't keep His will a secret if you are truly listening.

Developing Spiritual Oneness

In fellowshipping with other single Christians, our purpose is to develop spiritual oneness. Jesus prayed to the Father (John 17:11) that we believers might be one, as He and the Father are one. Our involvement in other people's lives should draw them closer to the Lord. Not an easy assignment!

We must learn the essence of holiness: adjusting our attitudes and actions to pleasing God alone. Daily obedience is the key to becoming sensitive to His voice and direction, will and desires. Being obedient results in a strong, positive concept of self, and in being a blessing to others. The result of two people who are committed to the kingdom of God and to encouraging each other in spiritual growth is a singleness of purpose, a spiritual oneness.

Fellowshipping for purposes other than developing spiritual oneness is the secular approach, which can lead to premature commitments, physical involvement, and broken relationships.

The most important reason to make spiritual oneness your goal in fellowshipping has to do with that quality which Christ says is to be the mark of a Christian: *Love.* Jesus said, "Love your neighbor as yourself" (Mark 12:31).

If we genuinely love someone, we desire what is best for him. Can there be anything better for a person than his getting closer and closer to God? God desires that we have an increasingly more intimate walk with Him. All of our actions, thoughts, and relationships should draw us closer to Jesus. If we play the proper role in someone's life, he will be drawn closer to God. The apostle John put it this way: "Dear friends, since God so loved us, we also ought to love one another. No one has ever seen God; but if we love each other, God lives in us, and his love is made complete in us" (1 John 4:11,12).

John says that if we love God, we will love others. The purest demonstration of our love for someone is our intense desire to see him more committed to Jesus. Wanting spiritual oneness shows your love for God and for others. Let's reverse the situation for a moment. Do you want others to help you get closer to God? Jesus said, "Do to others what you would have them do to you" (Matthew 7:12). If you love others as you love yourself, you will diligently work to draw them closer to God. The result of your efforts will be obvious: the two of you will grow in Christ together.

The Results of Spiritual Oneness

God is pleased when Christians incorporate Biblical guidelines into their relationships with the opposite sex. When Jesus Christ is Lord of relationships, Satan loses an important stronghold. He doesn't want brothers to know spiritual oneness with sisters. He'd prefer to see your emotions out of control so that you are incapable of making sound decisions. He wants you to focus on the desire for physical intimacy so that you will have to struggle with guilt and condemnation. He'd like to see you concentrate on selfish motives so that you will be in violation of Scripture. The Word instructs you to make a conscious decision to resist the devil. You can control your behavior by renewing your mind. Jesus said in Matthew 18:20, "Where two or three come together in my name, there am I with them." Spiritual unity gives Jesus first place and forces the devil out of the picture.

Body Building

Unity in Christ sets the stage for the ministry of edification, building up the Body. Romans 14:19 (TLB) says, "Aim for harmony in the church and try to build each other up."

Because men and women are, in many ways, opposites in their basic nature, ministry between the sexes can complement the differences. In fact, the Bible implies our need of the ministry of the opposite sex. Paul said, "Remember that in God's plan men and women need each other" (1 Corinthians 11:11, TLB).

Fellowship among members of the opposite sex brings spiritual balance. A woman's sensitivity can help to balance a man's logical disposition. Sometimes men get so analytical that they forget to be sensitive to others. On the other hand, some women can get so emotional at times that they are incapable of seeing a solid answer to a problem. Sometimes a man can offer the appropriate analytical advice.

If we desire an edifying fellowship with another, it is vitally important that we prepare ourselves. If our thoughts and feelings are not controlled by the Spirit, little ministry will take place. We can be in the right spirit by spending time with the Lord in spiritual preparation for the evening's fellowship. Imagine yourself asking the Lord, *How can I be used by You to help my brother/sister grow tonight? Please give me the insight necessary to help my brother/sister become stronger.* Consider an evening's fellowship as a ministry situation. God wants to use you to build someone up. But, it will happen only if you want it to and are willing to make proper preparation.

Relationships become a witness

As a woman and a man grow closer in Christ through

sharing and building one another up, God will honor their fellowship and use it as an instrument to share His love with others. As people observe the genuine friendships Christians develop, they will want to know the secret of rising above petty jealousies, bitter arguments, and selfish motives. People are always looking for something more in human relationships. Dozens of philosophies and theories are expounded today for creating solid relationships, but few are of any value, and none can compare with the type of friendship two committed Christians can have. So, today, when broken relationships are the norm, your relationships in the Body will open doors for you to share about God's power in your lives. Your fellowship will be a living witness of God's love.

Make spiritual oneness your objective as you fellowship. In so doing, you will please God, build one another up in Christ, and bear witness to God's love for a broken world.

10
Successful Dating

The wonderful attraction between men and women is always at work. You enter a room and fellowship with all of your brothers and sisters in the Body. Then your attention narrows to a few whom you most enjoy being with. And, because we tend to do what feels good, we would typically start spending our time and energies developing those few friendships. Among those friends, of course, are members of the opposite sex. And, when one of them is also particularly attracted to us, the magic begins! We start going steady with that person. We begin exploring increasing levels of physical and emotional intimacy. It feels wonderful, it must be true love!

Not necessarily. Doing what feels good can lead to a lot of heartache and pain if people don't make responsible decisions about relationships. Making premature commitments and getting emotionally and physically involved on the strength of mutual attraction alone are dangerous because the intensity of that attraction invariably weakens over time. And so, if people are acting on their feelings, what feels best at that point is to either escalate the relationship to a deeper level of intimacy or to trade it for a new relationship. In the latter case, one of the partners almost invariably is still committed to continuing the relationship and is left feeling rejected, used, betrayed, and wounded.

One discouraged man shares, "I've accepted being single just now, but my struggles come in trying to relate to women. I cannot remember having a positive dating experience. I've been hurt so many times. Even though I really want to interact with women, I'm afraid to risk an emotional involvement. There must be a right way to go about it!"

And another young man confesses, "I've found dating to be an awkward experience. These years of being single have left painful marks on many lives besides my own. I have related to the opposite sex by the hit or miss method. If one approach did not work, I would try something else. For a long time I had no clear guidelines and wished someone would offer positive Biblical principles for dating."

There are guidelines to be found in God's Word that can assist our development of a productive, positive dating relationship.

First, however, we must resolve a semantical dilemma. The term *date* is so versatile that today's usage has made it almost a synonym for *appointment*.

- We have a *date* to go shopping with a friend.
- We make a coffee *date* with a co-worker.
- We have a *date* with our barber/hairdresser.
- We go out on a *date* with an acquaintance.
- We *date* a specific person on a regular basis.

For the purposes of this chapter, we are using the term *dating* to identify *an exclusive relationship between a man and a woman who choose to make a serious emotional commitment to one another.*

We will explore the differences in approach and outcome between the secular concepts and the Biblical principles for dating.

Secular Dating: A World of Difference

Dating wounds sustained by Christians can be traced to the influence of secular society. A person living outside the rule of Christ is self-centered. Therefore, that person's relationships will be characterized by selfishness. He will be more concerned about fulfilling personal desires than seeking the will of God. When people crave personal gratification more than they desire to obey God, their lives, thoughts, and motivations run opposite to God's intentions. Relationships with self-centered persons tend to be characterized by sexual promiscuity, dishonesty, game-playing, jealousy, and pain.

Because the church at large has defaulted in teaching how to relate to the opposite sex, many Christian singles desire counseling about dating. They are confused, partly because role models for dating come from secular sources: television, movies, novels, music. If the Christian community has objected to these secular models, it has not consistently offered an alternative.

The voice of God has been muffled by the voices of society urging us to blend secular concepts into our Christian ideals. If the church does not reassert her ideals, secular thought will continue to influence relationships between the sexes. And tragically the selfish attitudes which wound dating partners tend to be the same ones that surface in—and destroy—marriages.

Not only can secular dating hurt your relationships with people, but it will also adversely affect your relationship with God. The link between our relationship with God and our relationships with others is so close that if we have a problem with one, the other is also hurt.

It is essential that Christians change their ideas about relationships with the opposite sex if they are to please

God. God is not honored when relationships scar us spiritually and emotionally. Yet, many singles in the body of Christ are negatively affected by their dating experiences. Sometimes they are so badly hurt that they begin to lose sight of their own personal worth. In fact, some single adults' experiences with dating have been so bad they actually prefer not to date at all! These are signs that something is wrong in the way we are relating to one another. When we fellowship together God's way, we are healed, not scarred, by relationships. The powerful and beautiful attraction God has placed between man and woman can be like a stream that promotes life and growth. Out of control, this physical attraction can be like a torrent that leaves damage and destruction.

Kingdom Dating: A Biblical Alternative

What the world models as dating should not exist in the Christian community. It is below the life-style of the light in which we are called to walk. We live by a different standard. However, what the world calls dating may be transformed for the single believer into a powerful instrument of fellowship. We do not have to play selfish games to have our needs fulfilled. We can enter relationships to find a higher experience, a three-person relationship: a man, a woman, and Jesus Christ.

Converting relationships from secular dating to kingdom dating resolves many struggles faced by singles, for it places those relationships under the authority of Scripture in three important ways.

1. Kingdom dating assumes the lordship of Christ. "Whatever you do," Paul wrote the Colossians, "whether in word or deed, do it all in the name of the Lord Jesus" (Colossians 3:17). And John pointed out that "if we walk in the light as [Jesus] is in the light, we have fellowship

with one another" (1 John 1:7). When singles acknowledge the presence of Christ and seek to honor Him together, their relationship takes on an exciting spiritual dimension.

2. Kingdom dating helps focus one's attention on others. "Each of you should look not only to your own interests, but also to the interests of others."

If both individuals in a relationship endeavor to care for the needs of the other, both will grow. They will stimulate one another to greater commitment and will find less need for attending to their own inner struggles. When singles make Jesus Lord of their relationships, they sense their responsibility to Him for investing in each other's spiritual lives. They are challenged frequently to examine their motives: *Am I looking out for his/her interest above my own?*

Paul exhorted the Corinthian believers to quit competing among themselves in their worship and allow love to rule their behavior (see 1 Corinthians 14:1). In the secular concept of dating, love rules the behavior—but it is usually love for self. The relationship is for personal gratification. Biblical love, on the other hand, always builds and protects (see 1 Corinthians 13:4-7).

3. Kingdom dating helps eliminate selfish expectations. Because secular dating is basically an exercise in personal gratification, both partners bring a set of selfish desires to the relationship. Thus the relationship is easily directed by emotion.

Jesus said to "seek first his kingdom and his righteousness" (Matthew 6:33). Dating with this intent allows a couple to genuinely become a brother and sister in Christ. If a deeper relationship ensues, the friendship which has developed provides a strong foundation for a lifelong commitment. If, however, the relationship does not lead to marriage, then the friendship will continue to be a source of Christian fellowship.

Therefore, reach out to fellowship with others, and seek their highest good for the glory of God. Let God handle tomorrow.

Whom to Date

Friends who are contemplating entering into a serious dating relationship will want to carefully evaluate one another. Here are some criteria which might be helpful.

What Women Will Want to Look For

Is he a man who wants to draw near to God?

James 4:8 (NASB) says, "Draw near to God and He will draw near to you." The man has the responsibility of guiding the relationship under the love of Christ. Can he lead you into greater spirituality?

Ephesians 5:22-32 tells the wife to submit to her husband. In order to do this a woman must trust in a man's sincerity and love toward God. Carefully evaluate a man's priorities and goals in life. King David can be the example here. In Psalm 27:4 he said, "One thing I ask of the Lord, this is what I seek: that I may dwell in the house of the Lord all the days of my life."

Don't mistake church attendance for "dwell [ing] in the house of the Lord." David was a man who sought the presence of God—His guidance, righteousness, and blessing. A woman needs to observe her dating companion's actions and attitudes concerning drawing near to God.

Is he a leader?

As we have implied, a man needs to be the leader in

a male/female relationship. In the Book of Luke, Jesus describes a true leader: "Out in the world the master sits at the table and is served by his servants. But not here! For I am your servant" (Luke 22:27, TLB).

A true leader is one who serves those he leads. The fellow you're dating should be concerned about your spiritual growth and interested in how he can lead the relationship in a way that pleases God. If you have to take the leadership, look out. If you have to insist on reading the Word, praying and sharing, then the man is not functioning in God's role for him as the leader. Picture this situation: Your date does not initiate God-centered conversation. He has not carefully planned out the evening's activity. All he wants to do is come over to watch TV and have you fix him dinner. If this is the case with your dating partner, he may be lazy. Most of you know when you're sharing fellowship with a leader. He loves the Lord and desires your best; therefore he accepts his role as a leader to make certain, as best he can, that God is pleased and that you are having a good time.

Is he a man who fears the Lord?

Proverbs 9:10 says, "The fear of the Lord is the beginning of wisdom" (KJV). Does the man you are dating have a deep and strong reverence for God, understanding who He is? To be a successful spiritual leader a man needs to have an intimate relationship with God, which reminds him that he is accountable to God. Respecting the Lord opens the door for wisdom to develop, and responsible leadership requires wisdom!

Is he a gentleman?

Treating a woman as a gentle, soft person is almost a forgotten quality today. Another way to express a gentleman's nature is being considerate. A natural outflow of a Christ-centered life is gentleness. In fact, gentleness is a fruit of the Spirit (Galatians 5:22,23). Men should be thankful for God's gift of women to enrich their lives. Special gifts require special care. Men are instructed to love their wives as parts of themselves (Ephesians 6:28).

Does your dating partner honor his mother? In general, what is his attitude toward women? A gentleman, walking in the Spirit, is sensitive to your feelings. He will show concern for your emotional and physical well-being. A Spirit-led brother will perform cultural duties of respect, like opening doors for you and having you seated first. When a man truly loves and respects a woman, he wants to do the things that display that regard. If your date is not a gentleman, the relationship cannot take on the proper form. Besides, you are too important to settle for anything less than God's best for you.

What Men Will Want To Look For

Is she a faithful follower of Christ?

Luke 10:39 tells us that Martha "had a sister called Mary, who sat at the Lord's feet listening to what he said."

Mary has been considered throughout time as an example of a woman who loved the Lord more than anything or anyone else. Her goal was to spend much time just listening to Jesus. His words were life and she listened and worshiped at his feet.

Mary becomes a role model to follow, because in all ways she was a faithful believer. Daily was her fellowship with Jesus. She was serious about knowing God and understanding what He wanted.

Is the woman you're dating or planning to date a "faithful follower"? Is her main interest God's kingdom and His will? Does she express God's goodness? If you haven't dated a woman with these qualities, you have missed out on the great time you can have with a woman who wants to please her Heavenly Father in every way. On the other hand, just because a woman is involved in church does not make her a faithful follower. Martha was busy working for God, but she lacked a personal, intimate, relationship with God. Jesus told Martha that she was too concerned over details, but Mary had discovered the only thing worth being concerned about. (See Luke 10:41, *The Living Bible*.)

Does she possess a gentle and quiet spirit?

A gentle, quiet spirit is "an inner attitude that seeks for tranquility, tenderness, and understanding. A quiet spirit is an inner attitude that is not easily anxious or uptight because it puts its faith in God" (*Discussion Manual for Student Relationships* [Glendale, CA: Shepherd Productions, 1975]).

And Peter wrote, "Your beauty should not come from outward adornment, such as braided hair and the wearing of gold jewelry and fine clothes. Instead, it should be that of your inner self, the unfading beauty of a gentle and quiet spirit, which is of great worth in God's sight" (1 Peter 3:3,4).

Much too often men think a gentle and quiet spirit belongs to a woman who sits quietly in the corner and speaks only when spoken to. Such a disposition may represent a boring person more than a gentle spirit. Some women are very outgoing; others more reserved. Women should be who they are. Peace is not always silence. A woman with a gentle and quiet spirit guides others to maintain a peaceful attitude in all situations. She desires God to be pleased and others to be encouraged. It is a privilege to be in fellowship with a woman in whom the Holy Spirit has developed a "gentle and quiet spirit."

Is she a woman who fears the Lord?

The same definition and characteristics for godly men apply to women as well. However, according to Proverbs 31:30, a God-fearing woman should receive special praise. Charm, by its very nature, is not necessarily good. Charm is wonderful when it is a product of God's love and the fear of the Lord. As the Spirit works within a woman, a Spirit-controlled beauty comes forth—a beauty that blesses everyone around. It is a genuine beauty that is not only attractive but encourages others to seek God. Those special qualities of spiritual beauty will contribute to the outward apperance as well as cause others to praise her.

Is she a motivator/exhorter?

The ministry of a spiritual woman in a relationship is often one of motivation. She encourages the man to achieve what God wants for him in his personal life, and in the relationship she takes seriously the exhortation in Hebrews: "Let us consider how we may spur one another on toward love and good deeds" (Hebrews 10:24).

In kingdom dating these specific qualities should at least be in the developmental stage. The intimacy of one-to-one fellowship provides opportunity either for spiritual growth or spiritual decline. Genuine Christian commitment for both partners is the first requirement for all these qualities discussed.

Perhaps you are thinking, *But my life falls short of*

these scriptural ideals. Remember these ideals can become practical aspects of our lives through the work of the Holy Spirit. Change will not come by our own efforts, but by seeking God. Desire to be more like Jesus. The characteristics expressed are the product of a truly Spirit-filled life. We continue to return to the same solution. The qualities presented above are a result of oneness with Jesus Christ.

Whom Not To Date

Whenever we discuss single relationships, the question of dating non-Christians always arises. The answer depends on your definition of a date.

For example, a cup of coffee with a regular dating partner would be considered a date. The purpose in being together is to deepen the emotional relationship, and to encourage one another in spiritual growth.

That same cup of coffee with a nondating partner might be merely an act of fellowship. The purpose would be to develop friendship, and to affirm one another's spiritual progress. This may or may not be called a date.

Having coffee with a non-Christian in order to become acquainted, and to draw that person to Christ would be appropriate. Unfortunately, people often start going out with non-Christians for legitimate reasons and end up by getting emotionally involved. *Christians should not get emotionally involved with nonbelievers.* To have a dating relationship is the first step in an emotional commitment, so dating non-Christians is not appropriate for a committed Christian.

A few years ago a woman we'll call Marie was apparently sincere in her desire to reach the world for Jesus. However, she began to date non-Christian men. When asked about this, she replied confidently, "I'm only dating them to share about Jesus. I've got everything under control."

Two years later Marie had lost the excitement she had once had about serving the Lord. She had fallen in love and married one of her friends—without leading him to Christ. A woman who had great potential for the kingdom of God was lost because a relationship with a nonbeliever became more important than her relationship with God.

This story is just one of many in which people have had their lives adversely affected through this type of relationship with an unbeliever. Dating is serious business. It is possible to survive a dating relationship with an unbeliever and in a few cases a Christian wins someone to Christ. But those incidents are rare. You can witness without dating the person, and without risking your own spiritual commitment.

We should remember that nonbelievers serve their fallen natures. Paul sent Titus a humbling reminder of that: "At one time we too were foolish, disobedient, deceived and enslaved by all kinds of passion and pleasures. We lived in malice and envy, being hated and hating one another." The nonbeliever operates from a different value system, controlled by an ego-centered perspective. God is not at the center of his life.

In any relationship there tends to be an exchange of values, ideas, and influence, as is the point made by the old adage, "I'll tell you who a person is by the company he/she keeps." Even if we were to have some influence on a nonbeliever through our dating relationship, that person would undoubtedly have a similar influence on us. We would tend to adopt the selfish attitudes, rebelliousness toward God, or worldly value system to some degree. That's too high a price to pay for any relationship. Christians cannot afford to date nonbelievers!

Neither can you afford to get into a serious dating

relationship with someone who, although claiming to be a Christian, is a stranger. People are not always what they seem. A dating relationship needs to grow out of a period of general fellowship during which you have observed one another in the family of believers.

Rosa's story is sad. She is unhappily married to her youth pastor's brother. He had visited one of the youth meetings. They met and started dating the very next day. "He seemed very committed to Jesus," she says sadly. "All throughout our few months of dating, everything seemed okay. Then, after we were married, he wanted nothing to do with God. Now, he stays out all night on the weekends and parties. We've never been happy."

General fellowship allows you to get to know people as they really are. Christians are instructed to examine the people who come to teach among the Body (1 John 4:1). Any one-to-one relationship involves sharing, teaching, influencing. A person you choose for a dating relationship needs to have a good reputation in the church community. Don't date non-Christians. Or mere acquaintances.

Terminating Inappropriate Dating Relationships

If you are in a dating relationship now that is ill-advised then you need to terminate that relationship.

Be compassionate, but firm. Don't become overzealous about changing your life and say something like, "Sorry, Charlie. Since you're not a Christian, you're going to hell and I can't see you anymore." Unless you can lovingly and compassionately explain your decision to live according to the principles in the Word of God, you will come across as being "holier-than-thou." And the response from your partner is likely to be negative, not only toward you, but also toward God. So be firm, but loving.

However, don't terminate the friendship you have developed with your partner. Draw that person into Christian group activities. Continue to care about his spiritual needs.

Am I Ready?

Not every single is prepared for kingdom dating. You must want to serve Jesus and His kingdom through your personal relationships.

Therefore, before you initiate a dating relationship, remind yourself that you are making an emotional commitment to another person. Identify the specific areas of temptation you will face. Ask God's help in advance and commit yourself to being obedient to His voice.

Next, develop a written set of standards for dating based on Scripture. Be as specific as possible about what is approprite or inappropriate for you as a committed Christian. Finally, purpose in your heart that you will not lower these standards, even if it costs you the relationship.

Kingdom dating is for true Christian fellowship. When other motives come into the picture, you run the hazard of adopting the dating life-style of secular culture. You must be so committed to the Kingdom and to your Lord, Jesus Christ, that you will not allow to continue a relationship that doesn't please Him.

You have been introduced to some principles about fellowship with the opposite sex that can set you free to enjoy those relationships. Now the only thing left to do is to follow God's Word and fellowship! Enjoy your fellowship with the opposite sex. Enjoy kingdom dating now. Dating God's way is an exciting life-style. "Unto him be glory in the church"—including singles and their relationships.

Practical Hints for Successful Dating

Planning is an important factor in the success of any undertaking, including dating. General questions that you should ask yourself approaching dating lie in the area of personality: what places, food, activities, etc., you and your partner enjoy. Particular questions, asked of each date, lie in the area of resources: Do you have the time, the money, the general wherewithal, to enjoy the desired dating activity?

If you don't answer such questions, you may end up as foolishly as the tower builder in Jesus' teaching about counting the cost of discipleship.

Begin your planning by consciously acknowledging God as sovereign of your plans. Your time together is significant and needs to be used wisely.

You should discuss your plans with your date. Besides being a matter of courtesy, such an exchange is only practical. She must know how to dress and prepare for the occasion.

Confronting Sexual Temptation

Given the practice of dating by the world at large, we need to hear Paul's word to the Romans:

> Let us . . . fling away the things that men do in the dark, let us arm ourselves for the fight of the day! Let us live cleanly, as in the daylight, not in the delights of getting drunk or playing with sex, nor yet in quarrelling or jealousies. Let us be Christ's men from head to foot, and give no chances to the flesh to have its fling (13:12-14, Phillips).

"Do not think about how to gratify the desires of your sinful nature" is how the translators of the NIV put that last clause.

To avoid "chances," to "not think about how to gratify" ourselves, we must deliberately plan. Planning creates a serene, peaceful atmosphere for an enjoyable time together. We can do this and still retain the spirit of spontaneity, which many people value. However, spontaneity must not be used as a basis for rejecting the planning of your dates or, worse, as a cloak for carnal activity. Remember the "deceitfulness of sin" spoken of by the writer to the Hebrews (3:13).

Paul addressed the subject of sexual temptation in his first letter to the Thessalonians.

> God's plan is to make you holy, and that means a clean cut with sexual immorality. Every one of you should learn to control his body, keeping it pure and treating it with respect, and never allowing it to fall victim to lust, as do pagans with no knowledge of God. You cannot break this rule without cheating and exploiting your fellow-men. . . . The calling of God is not to impurity but to the most thorough purity, and anyone who makes light of the matter is not making light of a man's ruling but of God's command. It is not for nothing that the Spirit God gives us is called the *Holy* Spirit (1 Thessalonians 4:3-8, Phillips).

To help you "learn . . . control," here are a few suggestions:

Men

Covenant with your eyes

Men, you can avoid sexual temptation by making a commitment to look at women only with wholesome intentions. Because the human nature is fallen, men often begin their sexual interest by "checking out" the appearance of a woman. Say with Job, "I made a covenant with my eyes not to look lustfully at a girl" (Job 31:1).

It becomes a commitment you make with the Lord. You must want to please God enough that you will make an agreement not to even *look* at a girl with sexual intentions.

Treat the girl as your sister

First Timothy 5:2 says, "[Treat] . . . younger women as sisters, with absolute purity."

If you perceive women as your sisters, it should change your whole attitude toward, and treatment of, them. Remember, you are going to have to answer to God for your actions. Maintain a Christian testimony by treating women with respect. Keep this also in mind: You are going to spend eternity with this sister.

Limit physical contact

If a man enters a relationship without expectations of physical involvement and maintains a deep respect for the woman, he can avoid a lot of embarrassment. This is not to say that all physical expression of affection is wrong, but we need to know where each of us is coming from. A simple touch represents a different degree of affection to different people—depending on how each one was raised. The same can be said of a hug or kiss. Talk this over with one another and together establish limits. Affection should be an act of discretion and honor to one another. Furthermore, be honest about your ability to maintain your self-control.

Stay away from seductive settings

Seclusion is not something you need in your fight

against sexual temptation. A warm, moonlit night on a secluded beach is too much for almost anyone to resist. It is better to stay where there are crowds, lights, and activity.

Women:

Dress modestly

First Timothy 2:9 says, "I . . . want women to dress modestly, with decency and propriety."

A woman should realize that her appearance has an effect on a man—whether or not she calculates it. At the same time, men vary in their response to a given appearance of a woman. No one sex, no single individual, bears the whole responsibility for the interaction between a couple. A number of factors are present.

For the woman's part, modesty is the best policy. Of course, it remains to define *modesty*. But to go any further than a dictionary is to enter the world of legalism. Two things will probably be adequate for guiding your dress: (1) What is the acceptable dress where you are going? (If "acceptable dress" is extreme, perhaps you shouldn't be going there.) (2) And what is your motive in dressing the way you are dressing?

Keep the conversation meaningful

The woman plays the role of the motivator in the dating relationship. Meaningful conversation need not always include God, but it should dispose the heart to an awareness of His presence. Ignore the stereotyped notion that a man doesn't want a woman who thinks. Use your head and stimulate the conversation with a knowledge of this world we live in. (Christians have a dual citizenship and each has its responsibilities.)

Let your date know that you're committed to Christ and that it is a privilege to share one another's company. Showing men that you have a high respect for yourself and for the Word of God will challenge them to grow closer to Jesus, and to desire your company even more.

Communicate a "hands-off" attitude

This is the same rule for a woman as it is for a man. Do not encourage frequent physical contact. A Christian leader shares, "My first Christian dating partner didn't believe in any other contact besides holding hands. I sure was teased by some friends, but I soon developed a deep respect and admiration for this girl's attitude. She became the example that I sought after in my future mate." Most men will respect and appreciate you for your honest convictions. If some men do not, you must reckon that as a cost of discipleship.

Applying Christian Principles To Dating

The most important part of this section is learning to apply the above mentioned concepts of dating. You cannot integrate Biblical concepts and non-Biblical concepts. In Ephesians 4:17-24, Paul says:

> I tell you this, and insist on it in the Lord, that you must no longer live as the Gentiles do, in the futility of their thinking. They are darkened in their understanding and separated from the life of God because of the ignorance that is in them due to the hardening of their hearts. Having lost all sensitivity, they have given themselves over to sensuality so as to indulge in every kind of impurity, with a continual lust for more. You, however, did not come to know Christ that way. Surely you heard of him and were taught in him in accordance with the truth that is in Jesus. You were taught, with regard to your former way of life, to put off your old self, which is being corrupted by its deceitful de-

sires; to be made new in the attitude of your minds; and to put on the new self, created to be like God in true righteousness and holiness.

The Word of God requires a radical reorientation of our minds. This reorientation certainly includes our way of looking at relationships. Don't integrate the world's way of dating with God's way. Instead, deliberately seek a transformation of your values and behavior to conform to the image of God that is being restored in you. Begin by consulting the Bible and asking God what attitudes about dating are left over from your old life or are imitations of the world's thinking. Through your reading of God's Word, you allow His Spirit to reveal to you what is right and what is wrong and to enable your adoption of a Biblical life-style.

11
Finding *the* One

An intimate relationship with a person of the opposite sex is one of the best gifts God gives us. In fact, in Ephesians 5, Paul suggests that an ideal marriage relationship will be like the relationship between Christ and the Church. What a treasure that kind of relationship is!

But how can we know if we have found the right partner for a life commitment? By listening carefully to God's direction.

Rebecca and I share the ending to our stories.

Ray:

A few years ago I took the young people of the church where I was pastoring to a youth conference in San Diego, California. For several months I had been struggling with learning to be content in singleness. People were always teasing me about being a single pastor.

After arriving at the convention, the registrars sent our group to stay in a local church, which (unknown to me) had as one of its pastors a friend of mine. In a conversation with my friend, he made a comment about my meeting the right girl for my life at the convention. Throughout the convention I had this unusual feeling that I was going to meet my life's partner. However, my first priority was ministering to the young people I had brought with me.

The second day of the conference I noticed a girl who was radiant with the love of the Lord. I soon discovered that this girl, Becky Knutson, was going to college only 10 minutes from my home in Orange County! As we shared, my spirit was drawn to hers, for Becky spoke always of God's love and the Holy Spirit shined in her life.

I tried to control my emotions, but infatuation got the best of me. I wanted to get to know her more.

On the last day of the convention, the speakers urged commitment to service. Even though I was excited about God's purpose for my life, I couldn't help thinking about Becky. Going to my knees, I sought God's direction and felt prompted to read Psalm 37:4, which says, "Delight thyself also in the Lord; and he shall give thee the desires of thine heart" (KJV). At this point, I became more aware of my desire to have a wife—Becky.

Before leaving the conference, I asked Becky if she wanted to go to a skating party with the young people the next week. All week long I daydreamed about her. I developed the weirdness and may have moved too quickly. One night over dinner I remember asking Becky, "Why isn't a girl like you married yet?" She didn't answer and excused herself for a while. When she came back, she politely ignored my question and seemed to have a loss of appetite. The rest of the evening I stared at her with dreamy eyes. I thought about her every day.

Becky must have sensed my weirdness, for she seemed to have little interest in me, other than to share good fellowship. We talked about it one night and decided to just focus on the Lord and minister to one another. Our relationship became established on prayer and fellowship without any physical expression of affection. Curiously, when all the romantic expectations were gone and we were just friends, we seemed to be much closer than before.

Then one weekend I took the young people on a retreat and Becky chose to remain behind. On that retreat, I began to search my heart for motives and the Scriptures for answers. I placed Becky in God's hands and told the Lord I would love Him and serve Him as a single.

Rebecca:

I had only 6 more months before graduating from seminary. I had finally come to accept being single. My life was committed to God, trusting Him to open doors of ministry.

That winter I went home to Texas to see my parents and to pray about my future. God had miraculously provided my plane fare, and I somehow sensed that this would be my last opportunity to spend quality time alone with my parents.

After Christmas I felt directed to return to California and attend a youth conference in San Diego. My seatmate turned out to be a Christian and we shared all the way to California. One of the things this man said to me was that I would soon be married and in God's ministry! Just before he got off the plane he prayed with me and slipped a hundred-dollar bill into my hand! I needed funds for this conference. Again God had provided.

My main objective in attending this meeting was to hear from God and to minister to others. The last speaker was a woman who emphasized that God could effectively use single adults in His work. The service closed with communion and a time of self-commitment. I prayed at the altar for a very long time, seeking God's direction in my life.

After the service, Ray asked if I'd like to go skating

with his youth department. That was our first of many evenings together. I tried to make sure that our relationship stayed at the friendship level. (After being hurt so often in the past, I wasn't ready for any more pain.) However, as we fellowshipped, we grew closer to the Lord, and, inevitably, closer to each other.

One weekend while Ray took the young people on a retreat, I prayed about my relationship with Ray. God reminded me of all the people who had mentioned that I would be getting married soon. He told me that Ray was going to be my husband. So, while Ray was away adjusting his priorities and surrendering his desire to marry, God was preparing me to be his wife!

We continued seeing each other, and one Sunday night we decided to share our feelings. We could see God's hand in putting us together for life. When Ray asked me to marry him, I gladly agreed, and we were married in June.

We were glad that we had become close friends, and that we had both accepted our singleness before God put us together. He clearly revealed His direction for our lives to us, and He will do the same for you!

How Can I Be Sure?

You cannot—and should not—decide the matter of the right partner on feelings alone. There are too many unknowns this side of marriage. Your final decision must have a firmer base.

Spiritual oneness

Spiritual togetherness must be a goal pursued by both of you. Discuss your Biblical beliefs and personal ambitions concerning the work of God. If one of you is not interested in spiritual oneness now, do not expect that to change when you say, "I do."

Necessary qualities

In an earlier chapter we discussed some important qualities to look for in dating partners. Examine your prospective mate to see if those qualities have remained. Be honest in your appraisal but also considerate, knowing that no one has reached perfection.

Seek the approval of your parents

Remember that you are marrying into a family. It is wise to consider the feelings of both families in your decision. Ephesians 6:1 says, "Children, obey your parents in the Lord, for this is right. 'Honor your father and mother.' " Generally parents know their children better than anyone else does. For real security, consider their admonition. If your parents are not available to provide that counsel, seek the advice of some older Christians who are familiar with your life and your relationships. Their wisdom can be a good addition to the decision process. The Bible says "a wise man listens to advice" (Proverbs 12:15).

Check your spirit

As you seek the Lord's thoughts on the matter, God will begin to speak to you about your decision. "If any of you lacks wisdom, he should ask God" (James 1:5). As you seek God, He will provide the necessary insight. Expect "the peace of Christ [to] rule in your hearts" (Colossians 3:15) as you are determining your course of action. Your feelings will become balanced and you can discern God's wisdom. What the Lord says in His Word, in your prayers, and in counsel with mature Christians should agree, producing in you a harmonious disposition about your ultimate decision.

Consider the circumstances

Look finally at the circumstances. If everything does not seem to work together, it could be that God is closing the door on this relationship. Sometimes, even with the best motives, we make mistakes. If our motives are pure, God will use circumstances to close the door in a final way. When God is in a situation, everything might not flow with complete smoothness, but everything will work out.

As Becky and I were making final plans to be married, we checked out all of the above items. Although we sensed God speaking to us, we wanted to be sure. We had the confidence of God's leading, in addition to the counsel and direction of brothers and sisters in Christ.

The Lord directs our lives with care. If He wishes to move us out of singleness into marriage, then He will work out the circumstances. You do not have to search unceasingly for a mate. Trust in the Lord with all your heart and He will direct your path (Proverbs 3:5,6), even in marriage. After all, marriage was His idea and He is still fully behind it. Ask Him to establish His institution between you and another of His own. He will do it!

12
Living Abundantly

"I've never been in a singles group where there seemed to be so much love!" Marcia commented after attending a Monday night *Praise Celebration* at Capital Christian Center in Sacramento.

There is a lot of love in the group because the 400-plus men and women who attend the weekly meetings are applying the principles of this book to their lives. As believers, they are committed to having general fellowship with one another, and to seeking one another's highest good. From this a sense of real joy emerges! Thus God's love is experienced not only by regular members, but also by those who walk in for the first time.

You, too, can know this joy if you decide to turn your life over to God. There exists no more fulfilling daily life than the abundant life of Christ available to believers—married or single. As your experiences and relationships are shaped by the Holy Spirit, God carefully works to produce an overflowing life, a life full of purpose.

All that prevents you from stepping into this spiritual life is faith, the willingness to believe God for all of your personal needs, the choosing to trust that if God has you single right now, it is best for you. Accepting your present circumstances as a part of God's plan enables the Holy Spirit to release in you the exciting power-packed life that only the Creator of the universe can provide.

Put all your life under the lordship of Jesus Christ and say, "Wherever you take my life is where I desire most to be. I will follow and obey you regardless of the circumstances."

Abundant, overflowing life is not just for the married believer, but for everyone who lives in obedience to God's Word. Do not expect an exciting spiritual life to begin with marriage. It does not start there. It starts with your individual relationship with God. And it's much easier to achieve a fulfilling spiritual life-style as a single and carry it into your relationship with the person who becomes your spouse than to achieve such a life-style *after* marriage. Accept the call of God on your life as a single person and initiate and expect an intimate, rewarding relationship with His Son. Jesus Christ reigning within your life can establish the attitudes you need in your relationships with the opposite sex.

The real message of *A Season of Singleness* is becoming more committed to Jesus Christ. Fellowship with God provides the deepest satisfaction a human being can know. "Thou hast made us for Thyself, and the heart of man is restless until it finds its rest in Thee."[1] Surrender your all to Jesus and allow Him to mold your life and relationships to resemble His life. Allow His Spirit to give you the abundant life, within yourself and within your relationships.

All the answers to your needs will not be found in the pages of this book. You will not become a contented single person by memorizing and quoting its principles. Such principles can serve only to draw you back into the Word of God. The Bible is all you need for fulfilling life, but don't take my word for it. Find out for yourself! Base your everyday experience on the Bible and see that God will never fail you. Abundant living comes as you make Jesus Christ Lord of your life and absorb the truth of

His Word. The abundant, overflowing life is waiting to be your experience. For God has great plans for you and your relationships during your season of singleness!

---

[1] Augustine, *Confessions*.